Ben is a product of the street and an English learner. He grew up in violence, but he prefers tolerance and acts in silence instead. He is a humble young man of a few words. He has no advisor nor instructor. Only his good intuition guides him on the right path before he decides to do something. He is also a machine of positive thoughts that can turn all types of obstacles into opportunities for himself in order to help other people.

He came to the United States in January 2017. He has no writing skills or diploma. Happy of being welcomed as a refugee in this great nation, he is considerate about his adoptive nation, and being aware of the injustice and suffering inflicted on refugees, migrants, and street children, he started learning the new language little by little before taking the risk to write in English in order to make their voices heard.

He would like to be known for the talent of a youngster of the street, but not for all the bad reputation people have in mind about street violence.

This book is dedicated to the refugee children all over the world.

Ben Dosso

Eternal Journey

Austin Macauley Publishers

LONDON • CAMBRIDGE • NEW YORK • SHARJAH

Ordering Information:
Quantity sales: special discounts are available on quantity purchases by corporations, associations, and others. For details, contact the publisher at the address below.

Publisher's Cataloging-in-Publication data
Dosso, Ben
Eternal Journey

ISBN 9781643788067 (Paperback)
ISBN 9781643788050 (Hardback)
ISBN 9781645365242 (ePub e-book)

Library of Congress Control Number: 2019914116

The main category of the book — BIOGRAPHY & AUTOBIOGRAPHY / General

www.austinmacauley.com/us

First Published (2019)
Austin Macauley Publishers LLC
40 Wall Street, 28th Floor
New York, NY 10005
USA

mail-usa@austinmacauley.com
+1 (646) 5125767

On the eve of Samba Diallo's birthday, a shooting's rain was watering Abidjan, and the invitation cards he had given to his friends fell into the plowing of combat. The gifts were flying in the wind.

Sky view—a bright city of bullets like the fireflies that were falling on the herbs and this city of Abidjan was devastated by a storm that nobody was expecting. The mortar fires of massive destruction were echoing everywhere like thunder roars in the sky and the earth was trembling at its turn. It seemed as if a plane was crashing around the house.

Before the horrible nights of bombardment of spring 2011, the city of Abidjan was peacefully livable and likable. On the other hand, inside the country, everything was ebullient, safe from an excessive community violence of a bloody Civil war. And in this combination of anarchy and general chaos, Samba Diallo's family got an unexpected visit in the middle of the night. The time at which the bars are emptied little by little. The gentle wind blows. The dried leaves fall. The silence controls the town. The sleep blinds the eyes and the dogs' barking penetrates the hollow of ears. A visit during in which Samba Diallo's family was ignoring the main reason. It was completely different from the many visits Samba Diallo had opportunities to attend or see from afar. Sometimes, Samba Diallo had no idea about these meetings. But during this last nocturnal visit, he was left for dead under the bed in the dark of his bedroom. Analyzing the degree of noises that was in his living room, he knew that the conversation was too stormy. And it was so hard to guess that this visit was a courtesy visit. Few minutes later, the conversation was turning down. But the shouts from outside could damage ears. This night was an unforgettable night for Samba Diallo and his family, likewise the rest of the population.

His genetic umbrella, his mom, who used to buy him all kinds of toys when he was still little, was shaking like a feather in the wind. A woman with a gold heart. Whenever Samba Diallo talked about his genetic umbrella's kindness, he used to get more smiles on his lips, as if someone was tickling him. A genetic umbrella that he had seen nude for the last time, unclothed entirely by the armed men. The one who was pampering him before they went to bed. The one who would wake him up in his pee and defecations in the early morning without complaining about these two toxic mixtures. The one who used to protect him from the hot and dry wind and the swirls from savannah and torrential rains that resulted in material and human disasters in working-class neighborhoods during the rainy seasons. Despite his exaggerated crying, his genetic umbrella always found sweet words, giving him a good reason to cool down his heart of the old Diesel engine. The one who used to breastfeed him when the employees of his stomach were claiming their rights. According to his genetic umbrella, Samba Diallo was just an aromatic reed, so fragile, that could not grow on dry earth without water, even if this earth was fertile for scientifics. Samba Diallo believed that his genetic umbrella could replace Santa Claus someday, to give some gifts to kids because for a long time, every December 25, celebration day of the birthday of Jesus for Christian Community, we see only the Santa Claus dressed in red and white, smiling in his long white beard like an old goat. However, it's not only men who are kind on Earth. Women are kinder than men too, according to him.

"I am not doing the eulogy of my genetic umbrella as if she was Virgin Mary, to offend people who did not have a chance to taste the honey of a docile genetic umbrella. That is not my main goal. But I am never going to know the faces of these ghosts with masked voices that were shaking my genetic umbrella's voice. I would give them a double punch in their faces for breaking my genetic umbrella that was protecting me against this hellish sun," said Samba Diallo, before joining a mourned populace on the public roads.

On the other hand, his dad, who was working as an officer in the military service, was always gone when Samba Diallo was still forgetting himself in the arms of Morpheus. Sometimes, Samba Diallo used to saturate his father's eardrums by curiosity with a bunch of questions during his days off about military service. He absolutely wanted to know more about military service. What would happen in the military camps if he would decide to integrate in the national army to defend the national flag color? He really liked this striped uniform like the skin of a zebra because when he would see his dad dressed in his military uniform, he thought his father was one of the heroes that he was watching in cartoon movies. Because his dad always used to tell him, "Being a military is to be a psychologist.

9

Being a psychologist is to be strong mentally and know how to keep secretly everything we see in military camp in a corner of the head. Everything that happens in a military camp stays in the camp." He also added, "My boy, you are still little. Be patient, when you will be older, you will know a lot about it. You will know what a soldier in mission is." His dad answered him, nodding his head. That dark face intrigued Samba Diallo. But by fear, the rest of his questions stayed blocked in his throat like Eden's Apple. He used to believe his parents to be protectors and immortal gods. Under their wings, he felt safety. Unfortunately, during the last visit, his parents were so weak, no more than a chick that was just hatching from the egg. Unable to defend themselves, nor could they defend Samba Diallo. Yet Samba Diallo wanted to be the guardian of national sovereignty and his genetic umbrella used to tell him to be a powerful man like Kiriku, as in his childhood movies, face the power of Karaba, the sorceress, making him play on word games. *Tom and Jerry* and other movies were fantastically funnies but the power of Kiriku was going to save his whole clan.

Meanwhile, the shells, the cannons of war, and grenades were exploding everything. The bursts of war were flying above their heads and the melody of gunshots sounded over the night. That was a great orchestra in the dark. The shouts of despair were the choristers to this nocturnal orchestra of terror. However, everybody was completely ignoring the key organizers of bloody festivals that were traumatizing millions of people and throwing them on the street. It's oftentimes absurd to dream of seeing a beautiful hairstyle on the head of a guinea fowl. No one will want to wear the hat of this human butchery, due to which the traumatized innocents were heavily paying for painful consequences in the terrors and blood.

"Sometimes, it's a docile goat that gives a violent kick in a stomach that we do not expect," said the madman sitting on the bench in the park. Habitually, everybody was peaceful living together and the city was very quiet in the early morning like a stagnant water in the upper neighborhoods. Apart from these, the roosters that crowed in the early morning, some government employees who were going to work, and the factory workers of this factory that was polluting the air at the exit of the city were the ones who would be awake. But unfortunately, that day, the roosters that used to wake people up early morning did not crow at the same time.

The smoky cloud prevented sunrays to light strongly. It felt like it would rain in next hours. The sky was cloudy. And an infinite number of people were running in all directions with whatever they could bring, to find a safe place. There were a hundred people heaped in a tiny, unfinished house and some people were soaking in the bloodbaths. The decapitated human bodies, some bodies were twisting from pains caused by machetes. Some human ghosts totally calcined were instinctively crawling to be safe somewhere under the sky covered by a smoky cloud. Most of them had crushed skulls in which bloody brains were coming out. Many people amassed like a bunch of woods burning from gas.

Meanwhile, Samba Diallo did not realize the gravity of injury housed on his stomach. Nobody was daring to make noise, thinking a little noise could lead them to the slaughterhouse. No one could talk either. Only the eyes could move where they wanted to move. No one could prohibit these eyes to see all these horrible massacres. To prohibit them, it was necessary to close them. But, nobody wanted to die with closed eyes like a blind who has his eyes open, living in an eternal dark under the light. The day and night were identical to their eyes if they were not located in time. No one could prevent the air that was penetrating their lungs and get it out.

The sun was very high. The shade was indicating it. On the central roads, the puddles of blood were connecting together and forming human blood canals. From that day of intensive bombardment, a big hole and a huge frustration got housed on Samba Diallo's heart and got lost in total confusion.

Journey

An afternoon, an old truck of a dozen meters long was slowly snaking in the turning between buildings' debris. It was moving at an average speed towards people squeezed in destroyed buildings. Few minutes later, the long truck stopped. People told Samba Diallo to follow them and get on the old long truck. Getting on the old engine was like getting on the last commercial vehicle at the Lagos market. Old people, whether they were women or men, young girls, young boys, and less young were nearly pushing each other to get a seat in the truck. Some people were climbing on the edges. Everyone wanted to get a good seat. Nobody wanted to let others get on the truck. Nobody wanted to miss this long unique engine. They were not able to bring forth their gallantry at that precise moment. Yet, there was no seat inside the truck. It looked like an old opened coffin.

After getting on the truck, the closing of the big door made of woods and some iron bars, maintained by some ropes of woven lianas, made an enormous noise. It was so hard to restart the truck. Few minutes later, the old engine started working again. Samba was less distracted by that commotion from the truck door. The long truck started heading to the opposite direction of the sun. And the journey began.

Samba Diallo sat at the bottom of the truck of about thirty tons. He felt sad for himself and a river of tears was flowing on his calcined face. He really wanted to die, but his human instinct did not want to see himself dying. He was traumatized and terrified. His mind used to reject automatically what his eyes was seeing. He used to refuse to believe the reality of these nights that he had endured. But the long truck was continuing to move forward toward the opposite direction of sun. The long truck was overloaded with men, women, and children who had certainly lost at least one member of their family and were squeezed against each other like fish in a fishing boat. No one had the courage to tell what happened to them. They were just looking at each other like a club of deaf. Probably, nobody wanted to widen the pain of others.

Suddenly, a shout came up from the bottom of the long truck. "Have you seen my sister?!" said an unknown person, seemingly the voice of a young man. No one dared answer him either. And the long truck kept tracking on its way.

After crossing many military checkpoints, the long truck started speeding up, and the dust started invading this human flock squeezed in the truck. They were leaving their hometown, kilometer after kilometer, and Samba Diallo was looking at the city through a small hollow of the truck. At the horizon, he could see himself moving away from the land where he had grown. The country of his ancestors. The land that was dirtying his shoes. He was moving away from the beautiful smiles of his classmate, with who he used to share a bunch of funny stuff on the playground in the schoolyard. The souvenirs of holidays. The sweet kisses and sweet songs sung in the bed by his genetic umbrella. The souvenirs of his genetic umbrella's soft palms on his cheek, like the softness of the sunlight at sunset, every morning before running toward his class. The long truck of a dozen of wheels was overloaded, and some wheels were already busted. There were no spare wheels. The diesel engine was getting heated up very quickly and the radiator also was a sieve. The truck apprentices were filling the radiator up with dirty water from streams. They did not filter this dirty water before filling the radiator. They were doing that almost every quarter of hour. The breakdowns were multiplying, resulting in many endless stops. Samba Diallo had no idea where they were going. But he knew where they were going was too far from his home. Some people were murmuring that the distance they had already rolled was the quarter of the distance to travel while they already journeyed hours, days, nights, and weeks in the same harsh conditions. At that moment, Samba Diallo was guessing about the number of months or years they would spend in this unsupportable condition before geting to this unknown destination on a stony road where they were getting whipped by tree branches hung on the road. Under the weight of his sadness and confusion, he was discreetly observing the trees moving. And he had the impression that these trees were also moving likewise as the truck. However, the vehicles on fire like scrap waste were not moving. Out of curiosity, Samba Diallo asked his truck neighbor, dressed in red and blue creased shirt, if they were going in the same direction as the trees. His truck neighbor looked at him nervously. And he made him understand by a nod.

"Trees are not competing against our old truck. Trees are not moving. They cannot move. Trees have never moved from their places, only the truck is moving," said the truck neighbor, looking Samba Diallo with his scratched face. Samba Diallo could not believe him. Every time Samba Diallo tried to watch the trees, they moved. But they would stop moving when the long truck was trying to slow down. In this swirl of dust and this dreadful heat like a 450-degree Celsius oven, Samba Diallo would drown in the hot sweat from other people. Meanwhile, the long truck was speeding up like chameleon that was watching his prey of the day.

After many days of journey, the tiredness could be felt on all the charred faces and the crying of kids were making some people mad. But they did not dare to say it openly. They were afraid of the reactions from the mothers who were protecting their newborns, as does a lioness. A small gesture of provocation could explode the deadly anger that the travelers had accumulated from the beginning of the journey against the long truck and its driver. Everybody was trying to avoid this spark. No one wanted to trigger the spark that could generate quickly. And the journey could be ended up in a forest. They could not say they were traveling in a rolling coffin in presence of the truck owner. As a matter of fact, the long truck was made for the transport of cattle and heavy goods. But the long truck was especially bittersweet for these hopeless travelers, because this necessary evil was moving them away from the city that was boiling in a lava.

Whenever the light of rays of the sun were getting devoured at dusk by the obscurity, the driver was parking the long truck by the side of road, on a slope to make easier the restart. It was not for safety reasons like a driver of a logging truck who was respecting the road codes to avoid an eventual accident. The driver was parking because there was no electric wire to power the turn signals. And the travelers were spending all night on the plant leaves under the moonlight, listening to the beautiful melodies from the insects, under the trees around the wood fire fighting against the cold. Sometimes, people let themselves be hopelessly beaten by the rain because of lack of umbrellas. Even if the umbrella was a metal weapon in the eighteenth century, it could be useful for them to cushion the tons of millimeters of water that were crashing on their heads. However, in the case of a breakdown, travelers were nervously struggling to remove the long truck in the plowing, using rudimentary means. In this humid atmosphere, the wet clothes used to dry on their bodies, thanks to the wind. And a harmful smell was invading the whole truck. The travelers could not breathe that air. It smelled awful. People who were allergic to this toxic smell and gas smell were vomiting all the rotten mangoes they had eaten. At the back seat of the truck, there was an old man in his sixties, with a bushy beard, dying of tiredness. His face was less smiling than a Buddha statue. According to him, the red monkey that had crossed the road at the beginning of the forest was the main cause of all the miseries that had struck them during the journey. None of these travelers had any idea that this old man was troubled mentally by the furious bombardments, but still had a strong superstitious sense after these troubling nights of spring 2011, or he wanted to cheer up the rest of travelers and make them laugh. Anyway, all of them believed in this myth of this old man mentally affected by the explosive grenades. But the suffering remained nearly as it was. The journey seemed endless.

After hours, days, weeks, and months of traveling in painful conditions in the long truck, they finally saw the light from the next country. The joy burst on all the faces and these calcined faces started flickering. But Samba Diallo was really sad. He did not want to get out of the long truck. The long truck was the only way he could smell his homeland. His tears started flowing one after other and wet his chest like a gardener who was watering the flowers. He already was too far from home. He probably would not see his toys anymore. However, the only memorable thing that he had brought with him were the only clothes he was still wearing that day. But, no one was seeing the sadness that weighed on his mind. Despite the unlivable conditions in the long truck, Samba Diallo preferred to stay there. He did not want to get out of it because the people around him brought him a huge comfort. Even if they were in a painful condition that nobody would wish being in, but the people who were at his side were reassuring him even more. He knew when the truck would be parked, he would no longer see those people. Even if these new faces were not familiar to him, there was a certainty that he would sink deeply into a new loneliness in their absence. Many questions were running around in his mind. *Is it wise to follow someone we did not know before? Is it the wise to live alone?* Who could better accept him such as he was? Samba Diallo, who did not know how to wash a fork. Finally, no idea came to his mind. Few minutes later, the truck nailed its nose in a monster traffic jam at the frontier. All the drivers were patiently waiting for their passes before crossing the security barrier. In this circulation dense of vehicles, motorcycles, and pedestrians, the commotion of engines was preventing to hear all distant conversations. There were some itinerant traders, almost mobile traders. Young girls of small size, sneaking out between the vehicles at a tardive hour in the night to sell some crackers. Samba Diallo did not know the exact hour. He did not have a watch around his wrist to let him know the time. But the sun had already set behind the mountain by the time the long truck was close to the river located at some kilometers from the frontier and the moon was strongly lighting, as if someone had put a power in it. There was not the eclipse of moon that day. On these itinerant traders' heads, the big metal plates with goods to eat and drink, trying to sell to the passersby in order to earn something for their families. In the plates, there were some freshwater wrapped in plastics, oranges, crackers, grilled peanuts, boiled eggs, and bushmeat grilled with palm oil, that was shining under the light. Samba Diallo's stomach was completely empty. He was salivating for meat. He wanted to leap onto the meat plates, but he dodged against heart because all his two pockets were empty like the vacant expressions of his fellow travelers.

After hours in the waiting line, the long truck finally crossed the first security barrier. Beyond that border of Mali, everything changed. Even the flag that was winging in the wind in Samba Diallo's High School yard, that students and teachers were singing national anthem to during national ceremonies, had changed its colors, besides the rectangular shape that was still the same. However, they were still on the same unpaved road, crammed into the same long truck.

Behind this artificial barrier that the long truck had just crossed, covered with dust, people started calling these travelers "strangers." People were looking at them as if they had got out of the deepest part of the Earth. The travelers were dirty after spending thousands of hours without taking a shower, apart from the rain that was washing and cleaning the dried blood stuck on their skins.

After getting out of the truck, Samba Diallo immediately followed people who were heading to an old storage store. They got in that old gigantic store and as Samba Diallo was drunk with sleep and the tiredness had weakened his whole body, he fell asleep in a second on a knitted bamboo bed and covered himself with a hand-woven mat. Every time he rotated on another side, the bed made a weird noise. All travelers spent the night in that old gigantic store where the insects were peacefully living, without fear, and the spiders had woven their roofs. The burst of the moon penetrated in the store through the rusty windows. Close to the old gigantic storage, a stream of dirty water was flowing. Despite the bites of the mosquitoes and the bedbugs, nothing could prevent Samba Diallo to fall asleep. He was so tired. He had spent thousands of hours not closing his eyes and fell asleep in a bamboo bed that was more comfortable than sleeping in the long truck. But, the bamboo bed was still less comfortable than the mattress that his genetic umbrella had bought for him. The bed that his genetic umbrella had bought was a comfortable bed with pillows and new blankets, the toys and the books with fanny drawings on the cover and the pages. In the bedroom, all comforts were there. Samba Diallo could not bring his toys and his bed when he was leaving his home. He did not know he would leave his home. Anyway, even if he had brought his bed, the other travelers would never let him get on the truck with his bed in such a journey. At early morning, when Samba Diallo had a bunch of traces on his whole body, he had the impression that someone had whipped him all night. He developed painful muscular pains deep in his bones. His eyes were swollen like the eyes of a tarsier.

The sun had browsed the quarter of the day, it was about 10:00 at morning, and the presence of travelers had spread throughout the new city in a new country. Some good-hearted women brought the millet grits to kids. Adults could untangle to find food as best as they could in a new city where they were strangers. That dish was a gift from heaven for Samba Diallo and other teenagers who were traumatized by hunger. Samba Diallo had never eaten that before. The sun was continuing its way and the misery was continuing to rain on travelers in their journey. From the beginning, none of travelers believed that the journey could take this long.

At nightfall, a category of men was watching a dance of *komo* (mask dance). Samba Diallo had no chance to watch that dance because of his young age. According to the traditional myth, the dance was prohibited to young women to watch at the risk of not procreating anymore, teenagers also. The old women could watch the dance because they could not give life to a child anymore. So, they could finally watch the dance without any risk. For this ethnic group which Samba Diallo belonged to, there was no separation between the traditional spirituality and the layman.

Everything was ruled according to the spiritual laws, from birth to death, which meant the soul of the human being having set a good example on Earth joins the world of their ancestors. Each family is connected to a totem animal for the respect for living beings; natural creatures possessing the divine plot help them learn the aspects of life and the rules of life and to be an accomplished individual in the society. The education system was very strict. Whatever the social status, everybody had to be submitted to this law of nature. The less affluent educated their kids according to the religious conception and their cultural identities. A neighbor could whiplash a child of his neighbor if this child disrespected his parents. On the other hand, the affluent educated their kids according to the religious conception and an Occidentalized vision. Over time, Samba Diallo started to get used to the new life, too far from his home country. It was hard for him at first. But it was necessary to find a balance between his old life on a scale and his new life on a termite mound. Samba Diallo felt a little bit comfortable because the new culture was the same as his genetic umbrella had taught him in his cradle. In other words, he was still at home according to the tradition, in the same Mandingo Kingdom that had been founded for centuries by their ancestors, except the accent that was a little bit different. But the mental line that had been drawn by the settlers during the world civilization that Diallo Samba had just crossed had its principles and its laws. It was the first huge obstacle. Even if he was speaking the same language as the other members of community, the same cultural identities and the same traditional customs, that did not make him a son of this new country. Being born on the other side of the border made him automatically a stranger to the law in the same community. He was less useful than a cockroach with this hat of foreigner that they had obligatorily made him wear because of a simple line. It was so hard for him to overcome this pain when he was seeing his identity diluting in the wind. And he started learning then that humanity was no longer united, but rather plural since the settlers made their divisions.

Samba Diallo was living with this pain among kids of his age. Kids had rather welcomed him as a friend. They did not want to know where he was from, despite the hate they were feeding against each other when they were playing hide and seek on the street in bare feet. That was consoling him a little bit about his internal injury, about his frustrations that were gnawing at him like a piece of wood in a termite mound filled with termites. From that day, Samba Diallo started to understand that the beautiful moments of life are to be a child. That did not mean that children think positively than most adults. Basically, children love each other much more than ninety percent of adults. For kids, whatever the gravity of their quarrels, it lasts only a few minutes and they reconcile themselves as if they were not fighting. And they continue their friendship. They quickly forget why they were angry with each other. On the other hand, the adults, no matter their social class, whether woman or man, their little quarrels are sometimes a nightmare for kids, and become a source of division of society. Samba Diallo was then wary of adults. He no longer wanted to suffer cruel words from adults that were ringing in his ears like a bell song during the recreation. He trusted the kids more than adults. He did not want to get out of the skin of his childhood. Because with kids, the life was wonderfully great, despite begging together on the street for finding something to eat. Samba Diallo did not want to grow up. He was really scared to grow up. He was scared to be inaugurated in this monstrous society after growing up.

All these teens full of hope, who had held Samba Diallo's hand, were from other cities and villages, here to attend the school year. In the evening, Samba Diallo would watch students coming back from school with their backpacks on their backs. He used to envy them for getting a chance to go back to school since the road to school was closed for him. It was in a dream where he saw himself in a school uniform with a backpack in his back. He did not want to wake up and see his dark shadow sitting in the same place, especially on the street. Even though it was written in the UNICEF decree that the school was for all children around the world, Samba Diallo felt excluded from that UNICEF decree. Also, nobody wanted to take the risk of assuming the responsibility of a stranger. Most of these children were joining their teachers, like everywhere in Africa, kind of informal school for not staying on the margins of education. This education that consisted of educating children orally or verbally, but not taking notes. It is fine to be educated. But the parents of these teens were sacrificing their lives to give a radiant future to their kids entrusting them to the spiritual guides. And these were guaranteeing to students' parents to give a higher education to kids. But, once children were under the authority of their masters, the reality was suddenly changing. The hell was opening its doors to them. Kids were becoming some *Gerebu* (beggars) against their wills. A source of enrichment for these masters. Kids were spending all their free time on the street doing the begging for their master counts instead of being educated. The entire collected amount served to fulfill the desires of their masters and the children received barely enough food to eat every day.

They were sleeping on empty stomachs and were fatally undergoing the misery and the suffering. And their masters were taking advantage of the low mentality of childhood at every moment of their existences. Their masters were making them believe that a disciple should suffer for his master and the virtual success would be certain in order to exploit them better. On same points, Samba Diallo and these kids had the common suffering of physical and mental abuse. It was these internal injuries that were uniting them together. And in this atmosphere of misery, they had become like a pair of buttocks, impossible to separate them from each other.

People totally forgot the rules of Sanakuya (alliance) and they focused entirely on the winning share. This fabulous alliance of the old days was playing the role of "pact of non-aggression" between the components of the Mali Empire under the reign of Sundiata Keita (king of Mandingo). All Mandingo clans were concerned by this alliance, the source of which was the valley of Nil and was spreading all over the kingdom of the empire of Mali. The real goal of this pact was to avoid the confrontations, conflicts, wars, and to calm down the tensions, even those present in the communities. The alliance was known under the name "kin relationships," forcing the different clans to assist, to help each other, and to integrate mutual respect but allowing them to criticize each other and to tease each other.

These alliances were existing as examples between some clans. It also applied between two members of different ethnicities. Mandingo Kingdom was maintaining this link. It was likewise for many ethnic groups. The prohibitions of the alliance were to avoid flowing the blood of their fellow men. But nowadays, they united only in case of a natural disaster. Everyone avoided the way of pardon and peace pathway. The hate replaced the love. The fraternity went out by the windows and refugees lost all tolerance. The liberty was buried under the laws and codes, only the strongest had the passwords, and the peace was crushed by these smokes. The flames burned the whole world. The sound of weapons replaced the roar of thunder that they were hearing when it was raining. The community wars were intensifying, and children became refugees over and over again and the incurable traumatism instilled in their memories. It became impossible to think normally and serve the society again.

In the hope Samba Diallo was dreaming to go back home voluntarily, but he did not know how to set up his return. And how to find his home after long time of trauma? It would be so hard. And everything was getting worse. He was not stable nor in peace. But, unfortunately, on January 2012, an armed conflict between the north and south plunged Mali in an insecurity and gunshots sounded again. This new war was involuntary pushing the thousands of civilians on the street. People were escaping the fire fields. They were heading to neighboring countries to find refuge. It was the day after which Samba Diallo never saw the band of his inseparable buddies nor heard something about them, and he could find again his home. The anarchy was reigning at that troubled moment. Samba Diallo was stuck. Forced to follow people again, avoiding the massacres committed by each other.

Shouting from pain when they got hurt to relieve their conscience, but when no one gave them a hand, they could only arm themselves to face what aggressed them. Everything Samba Diallo had endured was only the beginning of the hell of a journey he was enduring. Samba Diallo's journey got prolonged.

"Even if my journey could be described in a thousand words, in two thousand phrases and thousand books, and published it in more than thousands of journals, that could never make silent these chemical weapons that are roaring around the world nor make docile this aggressive world. I was born probably during a spring troubled meteorologically by a kind of malediction," said Samba Diallo, hanging onto a pickup truck. And he began again at that time a new journey opening the hell door. From one door to another door, he finally got lost in a darksome night of a hopeless journey.

In general, the wars definitively destroy most people during the quest of a safe roof and some people take advantage. In other words, the powerful people are under good solar umbrella lights and others swim in the hell of a boiling molten iron water on the road for exile. On the other hand, the war is so hard to understand when one has never lived in a war zone. They can't really know if the night claws when they have never traveled during a darksome night of despair. And what kind of an adult do children become when they have known only wars? How to rebuild a childish life in an excessive violence? And what future is there to be for a kid who knows only wars?

Cursed be the day when a kid loses his parents in a young age. Cursed be the eternal suffering that will open to him its doors, as the incurable pain will instill in his heart.

At dusk, where the sun was tired, Samba Diallo rushed into another pickup truck, a little smaller than the first long truck. He did not have the time to pack up his shabby life in a small bag. Anyway, it was already messy. It was his genetic umbrella who would bring order in his childish life, but unfortunately, his genetic umbrella could not be there at the time to bring order in his life. Meanwhile, the pickup truck was exiting the town and was taking a sandy road. It looked like the same road when Samba Diallo was leaving his home. And he had the impression that he was going back to his burnt home. He so happy and in pain too. He was happier for being on the way of return. He was so happy to see again his home, the land of his ancestors. He was so happy than all the other passengers in the pickup truck. He told himself that Almighty had answered his prayers. He told himself that the angels of heaven never let their children down. "The others' misfortune is often needed when it leads us home," said Samba Diallo, happily, looking up to the sky. He was nostalgic for his home. But, he did not really know where he was living before. It did not matter to him. He really wanted to be home. People were king at their home according to him. "It is much better to live on the street in one's hometown than live on the street somewhere among people who believe that we are a real threat and need to be detected urgently for their neighborhood's safety. We easily become a bag of human waste when we live on the street. People do take off the status of human being. Nobody thinks we could be able to move a mountain. We finally become a human waste. The fresh air remains the only common thing that its creator can provide the privilege of to breathe."

Samba Diallo could not see the sun anymore. It seemed the sun had lay down. He did not know the sun had a house in the sky where it was going to bed every evening and waking up in the morning. Suddenly, he threw a glance in the direction where the pickup truck was heading to. The high beam light of a car was lighting the road but both the sides were dark. He could not make out any difference between things. Everything seemed similar. Everything was sand. He could not see any more the trees that he had when he was leaving his home. The tree's branches were not beating them like in the long truck. There were no herbs also. A whirlwind of dust was preventing him to see where they were coming from. Samba Diallo felt himself in a big void. And when people told him that they already were in a desert, his big wish to go back home became very bitter in his throat as if he had drunk a glass of gallbladder juice. He wanted to jump from the pickup truck where they were heaped up on top of each other. But the high speed at which the driver was driving made him scared. The four wheels of Pickup truck were tearing the sand like an astronautic rocket moving in space. It was probably late, even if Samba Diallo could jump from the pickup truck, he could no longer know where they were coming from nor where they were going to. Jumping was synonymous to death. He would probably get lost. In front of him were unlimited sand dunes and behind were the same. Left and right also were similar. There was no a compass to locate oneself. Only the driver knew where they were heading to. The driver and his assistant needed only strong people and they weren't wasting their time with people who could no longer stand. People who were weakened from thirst and hunger were thrown on the hot sand like garbage bags. The young man who was accidentally fallen off in the middle during that race, the driver did not stop to wait for him. He just continued driving as if no one had fallen. And Samba Diallo began to imagine what would have become of him if he had taken the risk of jumping down.

Over time, Samba was moving away from his home. He knew he was born there, but he no longer knew where he was located. The hell on the Earth had opened its door to him.

Hell does not exist anywhere. It exists only when refugees are on the road to exile. And it becomes mostly harder when refugees are only a kid on the same road to the exile, and there is no one to give a hand to him nor defend him in the face of daily violence that claps him as "welcome" on the street. The environment that he frequents acts instantly and transforms him as it wishes so.

The first morning on the desert was another world. Everything was different. The violent and dry wind and a deadly cold. The pickup truck was passing some burnt cars during combats and many cadavers of people on this sand of Sahara who had fallen from thirst and hunger throughout their journey during this perilous desert crossing. However, when the sun was coming up, the color of sand was very complicated to describe. A beautiful morning but impossible to describe it because of moral pressures. Samba Diallo could see the limit of the sand dune according to the limit of his views. The cold was insurmountable, more than the winter cold. There was no snowflake falling there. But it was as if Samba Diallo was sitting on some icy hills because of the dry wind. His whole body was freezing. His throat was drained. And the skin folded during the night. Also, during the day, nothing could prevent the sunrays to project its burning light. They could make the brain boil. But the evening, the hotter temperature turned into colder temperature. And on this ocean of sand, some million tons of sand were superimposed in stairs like an escalator as if they were handmade. There were also all geometric figures between these impressive natural architectures and implanted away from the eyes was living a four-legged animal. It was looking for a weak prey where there was no food or water. The nature has its mysteries we ignore. We will never come to an end with discovering the many mysteries of nature and all that it holds. Impossible to analyze how this little animal was filling his stomach every single day. Meanwhile, days and nights were going by. They could no longer be counted. While Samba Diallo was accumulating days without drinking or eating, the hot wind was drying his throat and the dust was yellowing his teeth. It seemed the driver knew the dangers of desert already. He had all materials to protect himself against the dry wind that was making everyone thirsty. He was protected from head to toes. And Samba Diallo and many other people were exposed to the sun like solar panels. But lighting nothing. The driver made a step of kindness toward these hopeless by taking out a little quantity of hot water from radiator to serve the travelers a drink. They could not drink it quickly enough. No one wanted to let others take the first sip of water. A fierce fight got triggered, the water bottle broke.

Nobody could drink this hot water still. Their eyes were turning red, obviously from hunger and thirst. The journey was becoming a journey of eternity, and Samba Diallo was getting famished. Fortunately, in Samba Diallo's back pocket, there was a little packet of crackers that he had stolen from a store. He was putting these crackers one by one on his tongue discreetly. And his saliva was gradually wetting them. Then, he was swallowing this wet cracker, without biting on it. For his safety. Because if someone knew he was eating something, the other travelers would want to break his jaws and get these wet cookies from his mouth to serve themselves, despite the fact that it wasn't enough for all of them.

Every time Samba Diallo was fleeing different wars, he used to remark the presence of many men who were wearing blue helmets. Their uniforms were different from his invincible daddy's. He did not know where these men under blue helmets were from. He used to see them only during war periods. Probably the wars were symbolic to these blue helmets according to him. He saw them twice in two different countries. It was only war zones. He wanted to know more about them. He then curiously asked a lady who was sitting next to him. By one look, he could tell the lady did not seem ready to talk to someone. Her eyes were in the hollow of her face. She had lost weight a lot. She only had skin on her bones. She had the face of an old woman. Out of respect, Samba Diallo wanted to call her Grandma. But a doubt was hovering in his mind. Some people do not like to be called by their ages. Age is often misleading. Today, we cannot trust appearances. Some people look younger for their age while some grow old quicker. But the lady was dizzy, probably from hunger and thirst. And as Samba Diallo wanted to know what these men in blue helmets were doing there, he kept disturbing the lady. The lady could not lift her head. She simply answered Samba Diallo with a proverb "When a husband's beating his wife, there is only the neighbors who can come to her rescue."

Samba Diallo did not understand what she exactly wanted to tell him through this proverb. "Who might have the courage to beat his wife in this ruthless condition?" said Samba Diallo confusedly.

"Hmmm, you youngsters of today are really stupid people that I ever saw. You never grow mentally to understand life very quickly," said the lady. Adding, "These Blue Helmets like you said are United Nation peacekeeping forces. Their roles are special. They are unique and dynamic instruments developed by the organization as a way to help countries torn by conflict to create the conditions for lasting peace since its foundation in 1948," said the lady enthusiastically.

Samba Diallo replied, saying, "But I knew before, in case of a big fire in a housing, we were generally calling the firefighters to blow the fire out, making sure the fire does not burn the entire building. We don't take fire to blow the fire out. Otherwise, it could be propagated at a higher speed. But it could be unfortunately one of the biggest human stupidity and a serious human error to send blue helmets into armed conflicts in order to restore peace. Thousands get burnt under the watchful eyes of these peacekeepers where they are supposed to protect the masses. And these Peace negotiations always lead to revenge. The populations continue falling during each war like rotten mangoes at the mercy of insects. The remorse lasts only a moment, removing the survivors under the debris of the collapsed houses by chemical bombs. The dead would never be able talk about their discontents. They are quickly forgotten the day after the bloody disasters and people would no longer remember that huge alarming numbers." Meanwhile, Samba Diallo was also dying from tiredness, hunger, and thirst. He was weakened by the jostling. In this despair, they saw tents installed a little bit further away. All travelers were so happy. They were screaming with joy. They were hugging each other. It was a big relief. This time, Samba Diallo got a smile on his lips and his heart was a little relieved. He was breathing a new air. A new wind was blowing around him like the fresh air breezes the skin at the beach. Step by step, they were approaching the tents. Samba Diallo was so excited to jump from the pickup truck and take a seat under the tents. At first look, the tents seemed like a refugee camp. All signs were proving that it was a refugee camp. As soon as the pickup truck slowed down closer to the tents, Samba Diallo rapidly jumped, looking for a good seat under one of those tents. Analyzing the distance traveled, he thought he had gotten an Eden garden. He thought he was in an oasis in this desert. And the new arrivals' percentage did not stop increasing. After taking place, Samba Diallo thought that he was finally removed from all dangers that could push him to death. Few moments later, a man emerged from behind one of the tents, with a gun on his shoulder. And every passing second, these armed men were becoming numerous everywhere. All these men were dressed in Arabian traditional clothes. Their heads were also covered. It was difficult to see their faces in the scarves that covered their heads. The paradise which Samba Diallo was imagining was ephemeral. It was too good to be true and his big joy became a river of tears. They had fell into a wrong hole of exile during their journey. As a matter of fact, they were welcomed in a soldiers' camp. The armed group was different from the Blue Helmets, but suspended between two countries. These soldiers were all well-armed. They did not wear military uniforms like the other militaries Samba Diallo had already seen before. The refugee camp logo was written on these infamous tents. It was obviously readable without using pharmaceutical glasses. It was just a makeup to massively attract people in distress. The camp was full of all the influential nationalities. Their weaker preys were only teenagers who did not have any defense.

At first look, it was believable that these soldiers were only State's Islamic fighters, hidden behind bushy beards like Amazonian forest. They were united for the same goal. And to easily make the communication with them, Samba Diallo did not absolutely master his dialect which was so dear to him. Anyway, it was not important for these soldiers. But Samba Diallo's culture was still intact. No one could snatch it from him. So, he used to speak one of the languages that the settlers had bequeathed at his home during the human civilization that he had learned at school. Soldiers who could speak the international language were telling people what to do (they were forcing people to call their families for ransom). Samba Diallo could not speak any Tamashek alphabet (desert area dialect). Thereafter, an outbreak of violence rained. Many fathers had to undergo excessive violence. Many mothers were raped and humiliated in the presence of their own kids by these Lords of War. Children had only their little eyes to cry for their parents. They were crying loudly to let others hear the torture session that the soldiers were inflicting under their eyes. But the desert was not echoing up. After that wave of violence, kids continued playing on the sand as if they hadn't been crying. They did not care anymore about this different misery colors that were reigning there, these poor innocents.

As everyone had his turn of torture, Samba Diallo was waiting for his turn. He started shaking from fear. To dry his tears, one of soldiers found a method that seemed to him better and most effective.

"You better zip your stinky mouth. You are no longer the little prince pampered in the arms of this slut that you considered as mom. We are not here to waste all day to give you a nursing bottle. Give us your parents' address right now!!!" said violently the young soldier with a gun on Samba Diallo's temple, kicking strongly on him stomach. Samba Diallo instantly wet his pants with pee, without realizing it.

"I don't know my parents' address," said Samba Diallo, answering the questions that the young soldier asked him as if he was learning to speak. He could not connect the words together to make a correct phrase. There were only some vowels that were flowing between his wet lips.

"You don't know your parents' address?" said the young soldier.

"I used to know it but not anymore," said Samba Diallo.

"Alright! Look over there. You would be locked up, waiting for your family to send the ransom to release you.

Otherwise you will die here. Understood!?" said the young soldier with fury.

"Yes, understood!" said Samba Diallo sadly. He didn't even know who to call to pay for his ransom.

As a matter of fact, it was so hard for him to accept that someone had insulted his genetic umbrella. His genetic umbrella who bore him in her belly during the two hundred and seventy days with stomachaches and nervousness, who was so dear to him. But the young soldier had insulted her as if he knew his genetic umbrella in this dirty old job of the world. Samba Diallo could not break the jaws of young soldier to honor the name of his genetic umbrella. He felt weakened from being unable to face this situation, but not discouraged to not find a solution. His strong muscle was just a plastic that could not resist the pressure from the young soldier. He was just shouting as if he was in a funeral of a loved one. Moreover, among that human flow, there was a little girl that Samba Diallo did not know before. But some people called her Amy. She had a face of a doll and fairy ears with round beads. Her breasts had just began to develop. She was only a grain among a kilogram of sesame, physically endowed with doe beauty. She would have gotten all ingredients to seduce despite being covered in dust. But, observing her face and her expressions, she was just a little innocent girl who was smiling to the life if the war had not impeded her steps. But at her turn of torture, she had been raped by several people. That day, there was a muscled fighting in front of the door of her feminine private part. Not only raped, but also brutalized because she had tried to resist them. On the other hand, she had fought with all her might. She had flooded in her own sweat as if she had fallen in a barrel of water. She had shouted a lot. Samba Diallo was just hearing her voice in the wind. But Amy was slightly losing her voice because of the pain. Samba Diallo was seeing Amy's mouth opening largely and closing so slowly. He was brutally terrorized by Amy's painful shouts. The violence that they were inflicting upon her was stronger. The dress she was wearing was covered in blood, Samba Diallo thought that Amy had been brutally cut between her legs. She was shouting because of savagely losing her virginity. After a few minutes, she was silently shouting. Her voice was low. Samba Diallo thought she had become mute. On Amy's tongue, some sentences were coming out of her mouth with difficulty in a haphazard way. Such as "I am hurting," "I cannot anymore," "I am thirsty," "Give me some water," "Kill me, please," "Help me, Mom," "I need you right now, Mom, please, don't let me down. Otherwise, I'm going to die." Amy did not need to speak louder to be heard. Samba Diallo could decode everything easily that she was trying to say. He understood Amy's maternal dialect. He knew that Amy really needed help. He felt Amy's pain both physically and morally; he did not have a sister of his own and had always wished for one. He was living with a big emptiness inside him. He no longer wanted to play with his multiple toys. Sometimes, he used to blame his genetic umbrella for refusing to give him a sister. His genetic umbrella had already bought him so many toys to persuade him. But despite Amy's painful shouts, Samba Diallo could not rescue her. After her torture session, Amy was limping on her feet like a lamb who was on all fours. "If we were in this moment in a world of law, I could be deferred before a judge for the non-assistance to the person in danger. Because I felt guilty for all the violence Amy had suffered from," said Samba Diallo. He was blaming himself for the non-assistance. He thought he should have gone and helped Amy to avoid this wave of violence. He added, "Certainly, people could have transferred me to a prison with the police siren and lock me up behind prison grids. I would have served my sentence without parole. Maybe, I would have been forgotten in the prison." However, he was helpless in the face of this drama. He was just a flightless penguin that couldn't use his wings to fly out of the danger. He was just a little meat piece in a million of fiery embers. And all these travelers were locked in the mouths of the same carnivores that were devouring them. Samba Diallo could not protect himself nor protect someone else. Afterward, about a week later, after that collective rape, Amy was painfully suffering from stomachaches. And over time, everything got changed in Amy's body. She was daily metamorphosing from her toes to her hair's roots. Her chest was gaining volume, nausea and frequent urges to urinate. By signs, we could conclude something had been done in her belly. The young girl would become a mother in the coming months. Her belly was gradually swelling. Yet, she still seemed like a small child, no more than 10 years of age. While in the desert, water is rare like the marriage of a prince to a leper. Water was more valuable than the auction of gold in a market. People could beg someone to pee to get some water. There was no mineral water nor something to eat and her health was deteriorating quickly. Amy was losing a lot of weight and had become like a broom. She could not support a long-term pregnancy anymore. There was no a doctor there to take care of her nor a hospital. Only white powders used by soldiers. She ended up having a miscarriage. The monstrous cold at nighttime and the burning sun of daytime were insupportable for her, as they were for all other travelers during this journey. And one early morning, Samba Diallo and others found Amy bent on herself like a snake. Her whole body was frozen. She had passed away. And Samba Diallo and others continued their journey. None of these travelers were remorseful for her. All of them had unsentimental hearts, rougher than a rock. Because they were suffering daily from the same tragedy and were usually seeing this kind of scenes under their eyes practically every single day. Amy also had successively multiplied malignant diseases. Sometimes, when we can't save someone who is fighting between death and life, we can only desperately and discreetly wish the person death and for them to have peace in Heaven.

In some cultures, the dead spends some time at the morgue and a vigil before to be buried. But the day Amy passed away, her body had been thrown away a little far from the tent where Samba Diallo and the other travelers were living so as not to breathe the smell from the deceased like some hundreds of people who had already died from thirst and hunger. There was only a torn coat as a shroud to cover her face. The sand was getting hot. The barefoot travelers could feet it. For the teens who had thrown Amy's body away, it was just a kid's game. Because it was the day they were together unattended. Samba Diallo and other kids thought that Amy would join them later. They thought she was taking a nap, as nap is always good for the health. But, as the days went by, Amy did not get out of her infinite sleep. And she was becoming a bog body on the hot sand. Nothing rots on the desert. Any cadaver dries by the heat from the sand.

After this conditional release, the emotion of dying like an excavation under the sand had begun to install in Samba Diallo's mind. The punishment that the soldiers were inflicting to people was mostly harder because of the non-payment of the ransom that they wanted. Samba Diallo was designated to be one of the children soldiers because there was nobody who could pay for the ransom to free him. And as he was a little stubborn like a donkey for refusing to be a child soldier, his knees were scarred like the skin of a zebra by being forced to kneel on the hot sand. The blows of sticks would rain on him anytime he disobeyed the orders imposed on him. Samba Diallo preferred to die than be a child soldier; he did not want to tarnish the name of his mother. He did not want her soul to grieve and for people to dishonor her name, as in his culture it was believed that if a child took to wrongdoings, it was the mother who was blamed for the child's erroneous upbringing. He had already seen pregnant women disemboweled during the two wars that he endured. He had seen children slaughtered, hearts torn out and cut into smaller pieces distributed to the soldiers for ritual sacrifices to increase their mystic powers. Then, he was determined to not touch destructive guns. Samba Diallo could have become a criminal child because he only learned the school of violence throughout his childhood life. He could have become a ruthless child soldier terrorizing the whole world by claiming his life was already destroyed because of the disappearance of his genetic umbrella. But, this idea of revenge in the blood was

41

rejected by his conscience despite being insulted. The benevolence of his genetic umbrella had remained a guideline to him. And the weight of his faith was probably equivalent to his vision about the humanity. His soul and his humanism were weighing in the balance more than his monstrous ideas of revenge. On the other hand, even if he could explode the world with anger, his scars would not be treated. The maternal love of his genetic umbrella would no longer be brought back to him. Despite this clumsy and unhealthy ideology that people were invading his mind with, telling him that the real world did not exist on Earth, and that the world we live in is full of *kuffar* (disbelievers).

The sun was going down, Samba Diallo could see his shadow disappearing in the dark. And the darkness was exercising its power. The sky was not cloudy like other days. Surrounded by his old incurable scars and stretched on the cold ground, he was observing stars scintillating in the sky and the movement of the moon. He had the impression that he was swimming in the lavas of a volcano in eruption. He also had the impression that the earth was opening and closing in speed to break his vertebral columns. Everything was collapsing down around him. He thought the world in which he was living was different from the real world. That the entire world was piercing his whole body with a burning iron. That the sun was refusing to come up by his side and when it tried to come up by his side, it was coming up in the inverse sense. In this moment, he did not want to believe someone else's word anymore. He was rather believing the mental pressure inflicted by his oppressors. Samba Diallo was generally doubting about the existence of the real world. To his eyes, every single second was turning into a minute. Any minute was turning into an hour. An hour was turning into a day. Likewise, every single day was turning into a week. Any week was also turning into a month. Any month was turning into year. Every single year was turning into a decade. A decade was turning into a century. A century was turning into a millennium and a millennium was turning into an eternity. It seemed to him that the time had completely stopped. Meanwhile, Samba Diallo was not getting old nor his beard was growing like others'. Only lack of food was bothering him, and the thirst was devouring him from day to day; the journey was turning into an eternal journey.

Meanwhile, the insect sounds were giving Samba Diallo the hope that he was still living. Suddenly, he felt a crazy laugh come over him when he began thinking about his peaceful childhood. The beautiful smiles of his genetic umbrella were scrolling through his mind as if he was in a movies' field. Moreover, he thought a little bit about his invisible dad. Samba Diallo thought his father used to torture kids and massacre their family in order to build them a happy life. He realized now why his father did not want to tell him more about what would happen if he would want to go into military in his future. His dad had just told him that the rules were very strict, in addition he was still small to understand a bunch of things. For Samba Diallo, being at the head of any organization meant to save people and serve people who really required welfare, it wasn't to terrorize people. Over the years, Samba Diallo was undergoing the mental and physical pressures. Anyway, it was the only violence that he had known since he had left his home, what worse people were daily teaching him because of his lack of physical and intellectual maturity. And when he was coming out of his childhood bubble, he realized that being at the head of an army troop meant reigning with terror over the population. And terrorize people by spilling blood, especially the human blood, without realizing the suffering inflicted on innocent children who were over there.

It is really a huge sin to take away someone's life at an early age. In an incurable painful injury; Samba Diallo learned then to read people's thoughts inside of him. He began learning how to understand people in his own way. The outside world was violently aggressive. In general, in the battlefields, people kill to scare others, not because they want to kill, but they kill not to get killed by their adversaries. The powerful never sully their own fingers. They use children as scapegoats to do their dirty work for them on the pretext for providing them a better life. And if these street children don't do what they want them to do, they're threatened and forced in unimaginable ways.

The little tent under which Samba Diallo used to be during this part of his journey was a kind of prison. This prison was the most watched place. But oftentimes, there were loopholes when the chief Mohamed with the gray beards of bad preacher was absent. And as the surveillance was down that day, Samba Diallo took advantage of this security decline to meet some soldiers and make a friend. Making a friend was also like putting a pressure on someone to move a fierce animal's teeth out. In this camp, the eyes could see everything happening. Ears could also hear everything. But nobody could share a word with others. The mouth was a silent assistant, but an eyewitness. Samba Diallo had already taken the time to observe people one by one in this torturer camp. Inasmuchas, kids always react politely according to the good education acquired with their genitors. It is oftentimes pretty much the same reaction of a pet that reacts instinctively according to the actions of his master. Kids generally are easier to disorient psychologically. They become exemplary adults in the society according to the level of good education that has been inculcated into them when they were running in all directions in the garden. Then, Samba Diallo had put his whole hope on the smallest one among these soldiers because kids understand each other at a glance. However, it is necessary to be careful in apparently calm watercourses sometimes. One could drown easily if they do not know how to swim. This Little Boy was one of the must-have pieces in this Islamic Group. Samba Diallo knew that the Little Boy had put all his hope in an important place in these soldiers' leader's heart. By the size, Samba Diallo was a little taller than the Little Boy. But the Little Boy was more energetic physically than Samba Diallo, thanks to his experience in this group. By look and expressions of the Little Boy, Samba Diallo was perhaps a little bit older than him. Mathematically, the Little Boy should be at least fourteen. In school, Samba Diallo wasn't good at mental arithmetic. The mathematics was loving him still, but he never tried to be passionate about mathematics in return. He never understood why. Perhaps it was all in Samba Diallo's mind—he had made it into a red devil. However, his teacher used to tell him to make a little effort, that he could do better. He could have tried to understand math, but he let myself sink into his ignorance. Maybe he did not want to unconsciously honor Pythagoras while the arithmetic followed him every single day.

Apart from this idea, Samba Diallo did not have another way to escape this prison. He was mad with rage. He absolutely needed a potential accomplice to run away with. The weight of the pain was destroying him. And he did not want to die early with this severe pain in his neck. The stakes were high. He played his last card hoping to get the trust of the Little Boy. With their ideas together, they could eventually manage to escape this hell. Samba Diallo then put all the chances on his side. He used then the politeness formula that his genetic umbrella taught him when he was in the cradle. His genetic umbrella loved kids as if she was working in an orphanage. She was so docile. She was his guardian angel. With her, the life was a huge paradise where he could get lost. He could get lost through an imaginary universe as well. He did not care about anything his genetic umbrella used to do every single day for him. To feed him. "I want to be what my genetic umbrella was. When I grow up, I mean. Because she always was kind to people. She was as if she used to work in an orphanage. I positively kept her docility in a corner of my head. I wanted to be like her by drawing the path of peace with other children who were always blinding themselves in the childish system. But not this gentle genetic umbrella used as object of exploitation. Used merely as consumption for her function of biological reproduction marginalized and ignored. Used as a voiceless woman under the shade of her husband. Not, this genetic umbrella humiliated under the eyes of her own kids because of her right claimed. Not, this mutilated genetic umbrella programed for submission who does no longer live because of the social burdens. If I was a little girl, I mean," said Samba Diallo with enthusiasm. His genetic umbrella was his mentor. With this intention in his head, Samba Diallo took the first step in approaching Little Boy discreetly and surely. He firstly greeted him, hoping to get an answer. He was waiting for an answer to lead off a conversation in case of kindness from Little Boy. They could probably build a friendship. But Little Boy remained silent. He did not look at Samba Diallo nor answer his greeting. The mistrust of an unknown was a code already studied in this discipline. The unknown always is seen as an enemy. Therefore, Little Boy didn't have the courage to open his mouth by constraint. Samba Diallo thereafter returned to his seat with a heavy, shameful head. He was desperate. He thought the whole plan that he had long drawn had just failed. He thought Little Boy did not understand him. He questioned himself about different strategies.

Later when Samba Diallo was affected by the emotional shocks of his eternal journey, Little Boy discreetly joined him under the tent with precaution. Little Boy did not have enough confidence to do so when he was among this army group. Samba Diallo did not expect that Little Boy would join him later. Samba Diallo did not know likewise that Little Boy would have needed him so much. Little Boy greeted him in another dialect. Fortunately, Samba Diallo had learned some words of this dialect during his long journey.

"Did we see each other before?" asked Little Boy a little aggressively.

"No," said Samba Diallo slowly.

"Why did you greet me then?" said Little Boy loudly.

"I-I-I-I don't know. I just wanted to make a friend," said Samba Diallo.

Samba Diallo was a little bit scared. He thought Little Boy had come to hurt him. These men were not human beings anymore. But Little Boy didn't want to scar Samba Diallo. Little Boy then reassured Samba Diallo, adding, "I know you saw a bunch of bad things here, and during your journey. But don't be afraid, man. Be reassured, I am not like them."

Samba Diallo then breathed a handful of fresh air. Once again, a cool warmth blew his heart. Rapidly, a childish instinct began running on a good wheel despite the distrust. The two boys began then meeting each other secretly at nighttime without anyone knowing about it. Because of the bad looks from the chief Mohamed, Little Boy was already warned not to talk to someone else.

Day after day, the blind trust was setting up. They were becoming one and indivisible. The day was becoming longer and longer so they would meet again in the evening. When Little Boy would join him under the tent and as they became friends, Samba Diallo understood that Little Boy needed someone with whom he could talk to. And well, the mistrust was getting away, and the trust was getting in. The two boys could trust each other. They were sharing all the secrets and were laughing about them. Before leaving at night, they had promised each other to talk about their journey. Each of the two boys was in a hurry to tell his story. They had promised themselves. Samba Diallo did not close his eyes that night. The time used to be too long for him. He had the impression that the time had stopped, and the day no longer wanted to come up on the horizon. He lost momentarily his patience but was so excited still to be the first to talk his story. Samba Diallo could no longer wait to escape from there also.

After a long night, the sun's rays were rising at the horizon and the sun had started moving so slowly. The day was also going slowly. Samba Diallo wanted to put a rope to the sun to pull it down to see his new friend, Little Boy. Little Boy likewise. But Samba Diallo could not reach the sun. He was just a tiny object sitting on the sand dune more than a million kilometers from the sun. And when the sun would lay down after a long day, Samba Diallo would impatiently wait for his friend, Little Boy, under the tent. But, Little Boy missed the rendezvous at the same time. The time at which they were meeting each other. Samba Diallo was dying of worry for him and a line of less important words was invading his mind. He spent all night in a cloud of worries. Some days he would be exhausted. Samba Diallo did not see his friend, Little Boy. He did not also know what happened to him. And he could not ask someone else either. That had sparked a number of questions in him. They knew only each other by their faces but not by their names. One day after a few days of absence, Little Boy reappeared as if by miracle. It was a joyful night for both the boys. They were so happy to see each other again. They hugged each other. The emotion was a joy of the century. In this short-lived joy, they all forgot their promises they had made before they were separated from each other again.

The next night, they met again. They did not want to be separated from each other anymore. Finally, they remembered their promises. Samba Diallo remembered about their promises. He demanded then to Little Boy.

"Where are you been?" said Samba Diallo.

"I wasn't here," said Little Boy.

"Alright, tell me how long have you been living here?" said Samba Diallo.

"I live here, there are a long time ago," said Little Boy, taking a dose of white powder to refresh his memory.

"Really?" said Samba Diallo.

"Yes, since I came here, I always see the sun coming up at the left from my little tent and it is going down at its right. And it's a daily routine. Yesterday was the same ritual. Today, the sun is already above of our heads. The shade of my tent can indicate it. And tomorrow, you can verify it by yourself," said Little Boy.

"But, why do you smoke these weeds and this white powder anytime you speak? They are dangerous for health, right?" questioned Samba Diallo.

"Maybe these weeds and this white powder like you call them could be dangerous for health, but they are my companions of every day. Without these different doses, I can't live, I would be nothing. I could continue to breathe but not to be able to execute at the criminal orders from my chiefs to honor their hierarchies," said Little Boy. Adding, "Give me a second, the walls have ears now (looking outside to be reassured nobody was listening to their conversations). It's one of thousand reasons I find refuge in the drug to forget a little bit about the pictures of atrocities I saw before. The crimes we commit day by day under the reign of these human sharks. They are thinking only about their own profits. They don't care about the kid's shouts in distress. The innocent kids who are dying from hunger and thirst. Sometimes, in the hellfire they light up like a lighter.

They are destroying everything for conquering the world at the fanfare of machetes, rifles, and gusts."

"Have you ever taken part of a massive destruction?" said Samba Diallo.

"Yes, a couple times," said Little Boy.

"How did you get here?" asked Samba Diallo.

"Don't make me mad once again, dude," said Little Boy.

"I am so sorry, man!" said Samba Diallo.

"I don't want to remember that anymore," said Little Boy, nodding his head. And he murmured a lot and said again, "You know, dude, when the rebels came in my village, they burned down all the huts present. But, long before the war, there was a harmony that was reigning in the community. And at the evenings, the elders of village would take a seat in their hammocks around big wood fire, telling us about the funny stories of our ancestors, and the legends of village. Sometimes, we would fall asleep when they would still be telling us their stories. Their brains were quiet libraries. But when the war began, the rebels came to terrorize everyone for diamonds and gold that were a few kilometers from the village. And they put a gun on my shoulder. Before leaving my village with them, they asked me a lot of questions. I can remember exactly all questions. But I could never forget the last one."

"Which one?" said Samba Diallo.

"When they asked me to choose one of my parents I loved the most," said Little Boy.

"What did you say then?" said Samba Diallo.

"I looked my both parent faces, sweating, and I said them both," said Little Boy.

"Why?" said Samba Diallo.

"Because I had the same affection for both," said Little Boy.

"And?" said Samba Diallo.

"And the rebels forced me to make a human sacrifice before to be initiated as a child soldier," said Little Boy.

"What did you do then?" said Samba Diallo.

"I-I-I," Little Boy, cried out quietly.

"What? Did you...? Oh my gosh. Did you press on the trigger?" said Samba Diallo.

Little Boy cried for a long moment and they hugged each other again.

"But why you don't want to stop this life of child soldier?" asked Samba Diallo.

"I can't stop it anymore. I am already condemned to it. I am already one of rejects of the society. Who could be friends with me if there is blood on my hand? I do no longer know the road of my native village. I can't speak the language of my community. I speak now the language we speak here since they kidnapped me. Anyway, since they kidnapped us because you are among us now. You know what, dude?" said Little Boy.

"No," said Samba Diallo.

"I know only these regions covered with immense sand. Even if I went back to my village, no one would want to welcome me. People need a polite kid who is mentally healthy. My community would never want a criminal kid such as me. A kid who committed some terrible crimes. The population of my village and surrounding villages will always be living in fear. The information will quickly run throughout from one mouth to another. I will be the incarnation of an imaginary monster who will not exist nowhere, and nobody will get the courage to approach me nor build a friendship with me, and I will eternally sink in the deep loneliness. Therefore, I prefer to die here and dry on the hot sand with my weeds and my white powders like a leaf," said Little Boy.

Samba Diallo did not know either that Little Boy had endured too many horrible obstacles throughout his childhood life that would go beyond all understanding. On the other hand, Little Boy seemed psychologically free when he had told his story. His heart seemed relieved. It seemed as if he had just put down a weight that was weighing on his head that could not be seen. He looked relieved. In his eyes, there was a radiant joy coming out of his heart that was giving a fine smile on his lips. His face was lighting and his whole body was emotionally speaking. In his uncontrollable emotion, he then asked Samba Diallo if, like him, he had also come into the camp as a child soldier

"No, it was my dad who was going on a mission for defending our nation," said Samba Diallo.

"What? Your dad was a soldier like my senior officers?" said Little Boy.

"Yes, but not like your senior officers. My dad was defending the color of national flag," said Samba Diallo.

"There is no difference. A soldier is a soldier," said Little Boy.

"You could be right. But the difference depends on the reason why they fight for," said Samba Diallo.

"Alright! Call him then to free us from here," said Little Boy.

"I can't call him anymore," said Samba Diallo.

"Why? Are you killing me?" said Little Boy.

"No, my dad used to defend his nation but when the country was torn by the Civil War, he was considered as an enemy by the new power because he wasn't in the same political party as the new president," said Samba Diallo.

"Really?" said Little Boy.

"Yes. One night the armed and hooded men broke into our home. They massacred everything that used to move. Fortunately, I was still living but I was left for dead in my bedroom. I was so mad when I found out they also massacred my innocent pet that I loved so much," said Samba Diallo.

"What? Wait a minute. Are you going crazy, dude? Are you crying for a pet? Dogs that drag down everywhere in my village, eating in the landfills. Are you really crying for that? Shut up, dude, and talk to me about something else, but no more about your damn pet," said Little Boy nervously.

"You don't like dogs?" said Samba Diallo.

"I told you, don't tell me more about your freaking dog," said Little Boy loudly.

"Well, before the civil war, I used to go to school," said Samba Diallo.

"School! I've never been to school. What did you guys do there, make the bombs, right?" said Little Boy with enthusiasm.

"No, not making bombs. Every morning, my genetic umbrella, I mean my mother, used to wake me up early, forced me to take a shower first before bringing me to school like many other kids. Inside these big buildings, we were learning how to read and to write in the different classes, and on the walls the painters had drawn cartoons that were making us happier," said Samba Diallo.

"After school, would you become the Lords of War like my senior officers to destroy all villages and to terrorize people again?" said Little Boy.

"No, we become the exemplary citizens capable to rebuild everything your senior officers had destroyed during all these years of war and reach out to those who intentionally hurt us yesterday and banish internal quarrels. That was what they used to teach at school," said Samba Diallo.

"Could I be again a normal citizen to bring my rock to the edifice someday?" said Little Boy.

"Yes, we can be again new citizens, but we must leave this hell first and find a school to integrate in the society. My genetic umbrella used to tell me every day after breakfast time to be punctual at school and she had also added that the school was the future of a child. Wait! I forgot, do you really love your mom?" said Samba Diallo.

Little Boy got lost in a deaf silence, looking at the sky as if he was doing a session of hypnosis. Few minutes later, he finally found himself mentally and he was observing the stars scintillating in the sky, and said, "Yes, I do."

"Really! What can you tell her?" said Samba Diallo.

Little Boy aimed at one of the stars and said, "Mom! I know I can't remember your face anymore among so many faces I meet, but I do still remember your soft voice. This soft voice that forbade me to play with my games of empty cans at dusk. The same voice that was yelling at me when I was taking a shower in the rain, barefoot. Despite when the food basket was all the time empty, you fought in every sense for me, not to miss anything. You used to make sure, in utmost discretion, that no one knew about Dad's lazy side for the respect of custom and the dogma of tradition. You were the core of family because you carried under your wings the heavy load of the family. And I was the fruit from this union. But today I am the reason of all your shame for becoming a child soldier. I know you can hear me, Mom, even if you can't hear me. Mom, bitter taste of my tears scorch my throat and flood my eyes. My tears block my throat and my voice shakes. I want to see you. I want to touch you. I want to feel you. To be closer to you. I want to be in your arms. I would like to talk to you again. My heart is burning down like leprosy devours little by little the fingers of a leper. Mom, apart from you, no mother would have liked to dream of having under her roof a kid such as me who desires to feed himself with blood. Today, I regret it bitterly, I am a remote-controlled puppet. Help me to understand what I could not understand. I would have grown up under your hand. Grown up with your eye kept on me. Even if it often was a bad look. That would remain a look of a mother to avoid being a death machine. I have no idea where you are, but I just want to be accepted by you, Mom. And without you, nobody could dry my tears."

When Little Boy was talking to the sky, Samba Diallo had the ultimate conviction that he could see his mother among the stars hanging in the sky.

As the days went by, they two boys started planning together how to escape the torturer camp with some other children. That was Samba Diallo's first goal. Encouraging other teens to leave the torture camp as soon as they possibly could. And some kids got mobilized to flee the torture camp, those who still had the sense to escape in a great discretion. Everything was secretly being planned. Otherwise in case of suspicion, they would all get severe punishments.

A bit far, behind a wall of the sand dune there was another tent, smaller than other tents. At first sight, it strongly looked like a piece of sand deposited by the termites. The dust had transformed it into honey's color. To escape from the torture camp, they needed to be careful of this small tent. The smallest tent was a royal palace watched from morning to evening and from evening to morning. It was a dormitory for the chief of soldiers where they would bring travelers in and force them to give up any valuables and information they might have had about their families.

In the working world, the dusk marks the end of the work, but in the desert, the convoys of big trucks full of war arsenals and gas were coming from Algeria to Mali. From the beginning, Samba Diallo used to believe that there was a highway that facilitated the truck's movement. But there was none. While the high beam headlights of big trucks were making holes in the darkness, Samba Diallo and a few kids were planning on their escapes. The first attempt was a fatal failure. And Samba Diallo was punished severely because he did not know whom to pay the ransom to in order to be left alone. He did not want to become a child soldier so he disobeyed them, as his genetic umbrella had taught him to save a life and respect women, but never to take a life. He was electrocuted and whiplashed. But he could not denounce Little Boy. Because he still needed to draw another plan. Samba Diallo really needed to leave the torture camp. Nobody knew Little Boy was the central pivot of this escape. All the looks were on Samba Diallo. He bitterly paid the consequences of this escape attempt in the suffering. If the chief of soldier had known that Little Boy was in the *complot*, that would have cost him his life for betraying his hierarchy and the whole group. And he would be severely tortured before getting shot. Samba Diallo did not have the same fate as Little Boy. Samba Diallo could be just punished with a simple whip. Soldiers still thought Samba Diallo's head could bring some money to them. Yet it was Little Boy who had drawn all the escape plans like a surveyor who is drawing the plan of a future highway, because he knew all possible ways that could help them run away from the camp. They were so close to Algeria. After this punishment session, Samba Diallo had been locked up under another tent so as not to encourage others to run away.

Few days later, Little Boy came to see Samba Diallo again under his tent discreetly. The true friends didn't let each other down. As soon as they were together again, they started drawing another escape plan. One day, during nighttime, they tried to escape again at a late hour in the night. They were pursued for a while. Soldiers tracked down some kids with their lamp torches. But, Little Boy and Samba Diallo were hidden behind the sand dune thanks to the techniques acquired by Little Boy; how to stay hidden in case of an attack.

After a while, Little Boy and Samba Diallo came out of their hiding place. They continued walking together the whole night, heading towards the lights that they were seeing until early morning. Samba Diallo's ankles and feet were swollen. He had never walked so much like that before, apart from this long journey. He was so tired until the last energy. His feet nerves no longer supported the weight of his size. He wanted to try to walk on his hands. But he could not do that. This walking technique is not allowed to everyone. It requires agility and practice. Even though Samba Diallo's feet and left arm were hurting, he could not stop either. The only solution was to move forward despite the pain.

At dawn, the two boys were sitting in the cold, covered by a bunch of horseflies as a blanket. At the beginning, both boys used to chase these horseflies with bare hands. But, until to a moment, they were tired of chasing them. And these horseflies with their pointed mandibles were flying around the two boys to obtain blood. And when the boys chased these horseflies from left side, they would fly and sit on the right side. But these bites and stings from these horseflies were comparably less painful than the pain of the whiplashes that Samba Diallo had experienced before. At the same time, the policemen were patroling the city in cars. It seemed that they were doing the border control. Samba Diallo did not know what the meaning of a police patrol was. The car was coming to them.

Suddenly, Samba Diallo heard, "Stop. Do not move. Neither a step forward nor backward." These orders were coming from one of policemen by lowering the car window. "Hands in the air," said the policeman. The boys quickly executed the orders.

"Back up! On the ground and hands in the back," said the policeman, getting out of the car.

"ID control," said one of policeman, adding, "I hope you have your ID on you. Do not tell me you don't have any

ID, little snotty kids." One of policemen seemed nervous as if he was waiting for them. They got arrested for lack of ID and led to a police office.

And when they were on their way to the police office, the second of policeman said, "It is a big issue to cross another border without any ID."

Samba Diallo lost his temper. "What do you talk about, mister officer?" said Samba Diallo.

"I am talking about your ID, sir," replied the second policeman.

"I did not know that a piece of paper was facilitating people to move from a country to another country," said Samba Diallo. During the discussion, Samba Diallo remembered his school ID. It was only this paper where there was written his family name, his name, and his birthday with a numeric picture and more information about him, to his knowledge. That could facilitate this identity control and calm down this policeman who had twisted his arms in his back. But he could not bring it. Even if he had brought this ID, he would have lost it already somewhere.

At the police office, the policemen were a little bit indulgent with them than when they were taken in by the other policemen. Despite they had respected the orders, their chests were violently flattened on ground like some cattle. One of policemen did not want Little Boy to open his mouth to say something wrong. The policeman was threatening them to keep quiet. Little Boy knew him by his face. He had already murmured it in Samba Diallo's ear. The policeman knew a lot about all the arsenals of war that were crossing the desert like a line of camels. That was reason why he was demanding to send the two boys back to where they had come from. Meanwhile, the police officers were filling some forms out.

Few weeks went by. And the process of deportation was going around. But there were no more buses available for deportations.

One day, as there were no more people left to be expelled, the two boys were released on the pretext of deportation, but they were driven out of the city. They were treated like animals at the police office, they were not considered humans by the officers. And about two weeks of detention later, policemen were tired of feeding them with some rotten foods, and they got rid of them at the exit of Algeria. That exit of city was one of the smuggler fiefs. A piece of land where most people were dying in the Mediterranean Sea. It was the place where was planned pretty much all human traffic to Morocco and Libya and then the European coasts. Over there, people and different destinies were meeting each other and were sharing what we could call "human suffering." Some of these travelers used to call this moral and physical suffering "the reality of adventure." On this piece of land, people were suffering from exaggerated abuse. Those who owned passports were automatically confiscated by smugglers. And all ID were given back to their owners when they finished paying off the required ransom by smugglers. However, as everyone might have a skill for any job that he aimed, these smugglers had a particular art to persuade people. From the beginning, they used to relieve people through words as if their sufferings would be turned into happiness by a magic wand flick. The smugglers used to promise them safety and a better life. Like any human being who, when hurt and desperate, easily releases himself in the arms of someone who hugs him, who tells him some sweet words to heal his injuries. Throughout of this consolation, the smugglers would take advantage of people's mental weaknesses to open another big injury by plunging them in forced labors. From Saturday to Thursday, Samba Diallo, Little Boy, and many others were continuing their journeys in the different construction sites, working for the smugglers, singing their sufferings to the rhythms of hammers, shovels, trowels etc...hoping for a glory day like the elders who were singing about their damned lives in colonial factories, hoping for a change or for freedom from the grasp of the smugglers. Friday was a holiday. The day equivalent to the Sunday in other countries. This holiday was one time a week. And Samba Diallo and Little Boy were domestic workers with empty stomachs because of the burden required by the smugglers. This backward and forward on the stairs with cement packets of fifty kilos on their backs was literally destroying their fragile backs. And their wages were directly destined to the smugglers' pockets. The journey was becoming longer. In this misery what they were calling "job," some people who did not yet have opportunity to do their Hajj (pilgrimage) were profiting through their presence by rocking them, holding their noses. Samba Diallo used to get furious when he would see the smugglers negotiating with other people about him to work and was daily twisting his back for earning nothing for him. Furthermore, women and young girls, minor or not, virgins or not, in the same journey that was less important for the smugglers. Any feminine gender should make some money for them. No matter the way. Young girls were big sexual supermarket where men were entering and exiting like bees in front of their hives. All women adults and minors were doing the same job. Young girl minors were suffering more than old women. Young girls were mostly attracted by men than older women. They were often murmuring that they had become some sexual objects. But they could not say it openly. They could not refuse to do it also. Otherwise, they would be beaten with hands tied behind their backs until they respond positively to do this job loyally. It was the law of the jungle. Nobody could escape. They all were forced to laboriously work to escape the muscled deportation in the desert. There were only two possibilities: being expelled to the desert or keep working on the smugglers' account. Sometimes, behind any misfortune, there is always a flourishing business. Samba Diallo, Little Boy, and many others were so happy of being between the smugglers' claws than being deported to the desert. The Sahara also had become a cemetery for hopeless people. And to maintain their business healthy, the smugglers were dispatching their human commodity from one ghetto to another. From a city to another. And from a country to another. From mutation to another.

The convoy of human tide in which Samba Diallo was, was heading to Morocco. He had never been in this country before. Someone asked him in his dialect. He probably wanted to tell him a secret. But Samba Diallo could not understand him.

"Can you switch your language, man?" said Samba Diallo.

"Never mind," said the unknown. And the journey had obviously become most venomous. But, despite all this misery, Samba Diallo was hoping to go back to school. Meanwhile, their convoy reached out to the border between Algeria and Morocco. Almost a journey on foot, sometimes in a bus. However, the Algeria-Morocco frontier was ferociously watched by the border guards because of a border conflict between Morocco and Algeria for a long time. To avoid any control at the border, the smugglers were waiting for the nightfall before crossing the border. Apparently, it seemed that the smugglers were international diplomats. They had a strong influence on the state structures and in a society that the travelers could not minimize. The smugglers were always finding a ground of expectation with the border guards. People who were under the protective umbrella of smugglers were never on the deportation list. It seemed that there would be a black market between them. In the dark, Samba Diallo and many other people used to walk on a road that was deviating the barbed wire. The guards and the bad dogs were posted at the border. The smugglers did not care about police, likewise Little Boy. But Samba Diallo would shake whenever he heard the word "police." The deviation was an old tunnel where a large population of bats and spider roofs were peacefully living. A souvenir bequeathed by the two world wars where these travelers were squeezing each other by the hundreds like Fossae. The border crossing was in a dark to avoid any suspicion. That could push down the flourishing business between the authorities and smugglers. Before leaving these travelers in the count of other smugglers, the first ones were searching them 'til their anus looking for any penny.

Morocco

A new sun was rising at the horizon above the buildings with red facades of Morocco, seaside cities of many wild cats. The generosity was over there. Samba Diallo and Little Boy and other travelers in their journeys couldn't die from hunger thanks to bread donations. Despite the poverty and the mixture of the hypocrisy, some people could give a hand to others for the respect of their tradition. But some people were making donations because of the pressure of the cultural myths. Others, by contrast, did so by generosity. The population was charitable despite an exaggerated racism. The journey could be finished there. Because the two boys, Samba Diallo and Little Boy, were immediately fascinated by the architectures with red facades and the traditional potteries unique in its kind. The cultural landscape of Berber sounds and dances was some spectacle, rich in poetry colors. The folklore stories across the whole country and its famous *riads*, traditional Moroccan house or palace with an interior garden or courtyard. The relieving heat of the Turkish bath. The beautiful beaches with fine sands, the beauty of the landscape and the blue color of the Mediterranean Sea. As for the cuisine, it was a Mediterranean cuisine characterized by the variety of dishes, mainly Arab and Berber origin with a Jewish influence. It was also reflecting the history of the country and its people who settle there: orange salad scented with cinnamon, the spicy tajine, and the unforgettable appetizing savor of couscous shared every Friday after the prayer of *Jummah* (Friday prayer). Furthermore, Samba Diallo was passionate about the kisses on the forehead of old people for the cultural respect of elder people and the kisses on the king's hand for the majestic respect for all symbols that represent the kingdom, but he was suddenly upset by the young girls left behind after a sexual aggression. This category of young girls marginalized who no longer belonged to the society because they were no longer virgin and these many elderly people left behind because they were no longer useful to the society. And he wanted to settle, hoping to go back to school with Little Boy if his own decisions were his. In his backpack of a beggar, there were some scattered dreams, some melancholy poetic phrases, and rhymes filled with misspellings that he thought to take care of it.

But Samba Diallo's dirty mouth of a negro and his faded eyes that were making him want to dream were not welcomed. The fresh wind was poisoned of a huge wave of discrimination. Samba Diallo's color had a meaning. The masculine name given to people of his color was Azi. The feminine of Azi was Azia and the docile synonym of all these names was "*mon ami*" and "*mon amia*," all derogatory terms. In the street, everyone used to hold their noses not to breathe the wind around him, believing he did not know the cost of a water drop from the pump. Yet he wasn't stinking like the infamous perfume of mongoose. The two boys were ashamed to walk on the street and to approach other children of their ages. Even if other kids wanted to play with Samba Diallo, their parents would impose. They used to scare their children not to play with a sub-Saharan kid. Almost all of these people did not recognize an African. They would forget that Maghreb was not located on another continent nor a Western province. One needn't necessarily be a psychologist to know the mental traumatism that Samba Diallo and Little Boy were suffering from.

In the city, the police reprisals were horrible. People were running to escape the humiliations and the suicidal deportations. Meanwhile, the smugglers were selling the European dream to refugees where everything was wonderful like a garden of flower. This imaginary fruit was influencing many people to escape the police violence, hoping to find the eventual peace in Europe. This influence of smugglers pushed a big pressure on Samba Diallo's dream to find a public school. On the other hand, Little Boy could not read nor write. He had difficulty writing his name, saying with an embarrassed shrug that he had never touched a pen in his lifetime. He was content to the little that Samba Diallo had learned at school. It was so hard for him to spell the letters. He had had a funny mouth when he was trying to spell words. The two boys, Samba Diallo and Little Boy, had the same goal to go back to school. But, at that time, the system of public schools couldn't allow refugees children to go back to school because of the administrative issues. And under the dominative pressure of smugglers, the two boys re-packed their bags to confront a new perilous journey to Nador, a city located in northeast in Morocco. However, Samba Diallo's journey had already lasted more than three years between the hammer and the anvil. More than thirty-six months of suffering. More than one hundred and forty-four weeks of begging. More than a thousand days of insomnia, of mental depression in the different colors of urban violence. At the same time, Samba Diallo was crazily in love, having so much affection for this Cherifian Kingdom despite people were confiscated and ripped off all their precious things with machetes. And the authorities used to trample his complaints under his eyes, the identity perverts who used to tell him that this host country was not his. Samba Diallo could give everything to settle there. He did what he could do to be accepted in this community. But all his effort flew into nothingness.

"Even if I should leave here, I would leave without ever being able to leave because I would never be gone, my heart would be with these old ladies who had already carved their generosity on my heart," said Samba Diallo, lamenting.

They finally got Nador. There were thousands of travelers who had come from sub-Saharan countries and Middle East. They were from many different countries where the war arsenals were blowing up everything. Before reaching Nador, it was useless to go to the bus station. The tickets were not sold to the travelers like Samba Diallo and Little Boy. Then, they were waiting for the departure of the train in their different hiding places and hung on the wagon like bats. The train was transporting the charcoals for the factory located at the seaside. The train was arriving at its destination between the first call of the morning prayer and the sunrise. However, Samba Diallo, Little Boy, and others were getting ready, jumping down from the train before it slowed down to escape the punches from the railway guards. And the unfortunate ones who were awkwardly jumping on wrong feet were rapidly getting crushed by the train in speed. Nevertheless, they left the wounded ones at the end of the main road so that the Red Cross could take care of them. And the survivors of this journey used to track on the way of their safety and economy issues. All these travelers were generally heading to Gurugu Mountain, a rocky hill, culminating at nine hundred meters near to the lagoon of Nador, Beni Ansar, and Melilla. Gurugu Mountain was also a refuge for hundreds of refugees and economic migrants waiting desperately to cross into Europe. But the frontier was muscly watched by the policemen placed in any corner. And the arrests used to multiply. It was the economic migrants' hunting. But to reach it, the travelers risked death and injury by climbing on a heavily fortified fence which encircles the territory, or out at sea as they tried to swim through the dark waters to reach the Spanish beach. And the unfortunate ones as human shields were living at the feet of the misery trees and forgotten among crawling reptiles in forest where the body lice were making some button belts around our pelvis and the ticks were housing under their armpits, and they were becoming exoskeletons of arthropods in which these insects used to sojourn, fleeing their stalker predators. It was the same, winter as summer. In addition, to get water, these journeymen walked a long distance on the rocks to reach out the cave at a dozen miles, likewise getting the wood to fight against the cold. It was a necessity because they couldn't go to the downtown in fear of getting deported to the desert. While they were devoured by the monster cold of the winter and the rain mixed with the wind were worsening their living conditions. Regarding the food, these travelers were doing their food shopping at nightfall in the urban dumps by imposing the jungle law to the hundreds of fat cats that were the owners of public dumps to getting food. It was a solidary group sharing the same misfortunes and sufferings under the shelters. The fellow travelers who only knew each other by their nicknames, despite their cultural and ethnic diversities, were a family in a miserly atmosphere. A jungle where different bitter stories were making collisions. Each shelter housed a bitter story, it was hard to listen to the whole story to the end without tearing up a little. A long refugees' journey, fleeing the heavy pressure from the police, throwing some vulgar words in the wind to relieve their hearts. Sometimes, the different communities were fighting each other because of treason and the youngest like Samba Diallo, Little Boy, and a dozen others were painfully suffering from it. But, a bit far from this misery coffin, there was Melilla, a tiny autonomous Spanish enclave on the north coast of Morocco, one of the few lands into the European Union and the gateway to Europe coming from Africa. This border was also the line that was dividing the world of the intelligent people and the world of the savage people, separated by an iron curtain of barbed wire, iridescent razor blade, noise motion detectors, the night vision cameras, watchtowers, and a tireless patrol of police. Police dogs could stop these travelers in a split second in full speed with their enormous power and the deafening noises from the helicopters in the sky were enough to bring them out of their hiding places. The shepherds were snitching on those trying to smuggle out of the area by tipping off the police. They knew most of the hiding places of these travelers. Throughout these patrols of sweep, all shelters were burnt down by auxiliary forces, militaries and national police, bringing the good things useful for them and they used to set up a theatrical scene, accusing the travelers for burning to the ground their own shelters to make up their carnages. The reprisals were daily. All these sufferings were pushing people to climb desperately this triple fencing system of seven meters that were hanging on dozen kilometers. Samba Diallo and Little Boy were only simple dwarfs under this wall with barbed wire of seven meters in length. And under the threat of border guards, some of these travelers had their throat slit by rolls of barbed wire. A human tide in herds like an impressive buffalo herd that could uproot all the carrots of the peasants in their passage. Moreover, almost all of them were literally suffering from the last degree of literacy. On the other hand, in front of the barrier the border guards of Europe were mortally beating them with the blows of batons, cudgeling to death, who were being financed over thirty million Euros to prevent these children asylum seekers to be reeducated. Some of them were corporally beaten at death for touching the barrier. And the police cars were deployed everywhere. The sirens of police were wailing as if these travelers had just committed an attack. The lucky ones of these travelers had broken limbs. Front of the international medias, the Guardia Civil (Spanish) was rejecting all these wrongdoings of the ill-treatments of human, accusing the Moroccan auxiliary forces, and the Moroccan Auxiliary forces were also rejecting all charges. None of these forces wanted to accept accusations of beating people to death. Yet these travelers were beaten on the European soil before being thrown by the small door of iron curtains. And once on the Moroccan soil, police used to achieve the rest of dirty work by driving their vans in the crowd, and the unlucky ones of these travelers were perishing before the beginning of the suicidal deportations of the survivors in the buses. Both camps were accusing each other of disseminating these charges. Yet both camps

71

were implicated in these abuses. Europe did not need economic migrations on its soil. It did not want to welcome all misery of entire world. However, the same Europe was daily advocating education for all children without distinction. Who are they manipulating then with their children's rights?

Baba (Daddy in Arabic) was working in one of the countries of the defenders of Children Rights, Human Rights, all kinds of human rights and animal rights from Monday to Friday. Even if Baba was not the father of all these travelers, they used to call him Baba due to his kindness and generosity and the respect of his humanitarian vision. Baba was leaving from his work at 3:00 pm, local time. Every Friday afternoon at the same time, he used to think about these travelers under these trees of misery. On his way from his work, he used to load his grey Peugeot car with pieces of bread, jams, tea, and sugar packages, some grams of rice, paracetamols, and some blankets. Baba used to do this great donation every Friday at the same time as he could. Every Friday afternoon, Baba knew that the travelers were waiting for him at the foot of this hill, and the travelers were also hoping that Baba would bring new feed coming from Europe. These little packages of food could not last for the whole week, but they were an oasis for these travelers under these miserly trees because this food was completely different from the rotten food that they picked up from the bins on other side of the town. But Baba's generosity was viewed by a bad eye by the local police. Police used to reproach him for encouraging immigration without knowing his motivation. Yet Baba used to help people who were starving and children who were dying in cold in the deadly winter weather. Moreover, Baba was receiving summons for helping travelers. He used to tell travelers about these summons. His car was pursued by the police cars when he was coming from work. The police used to chase the travelers who would be waiting for Baba. As Baba could no longer share the food with the travelers, he switched his schedule to continue helping the travelers in their long journey. As usual, he was loading a small wheelbarrow with food and was silently pushing it to the new place to share with the travelers the little he had. Meanwhile, the economic migrant hunts and these deportations in the desert the travelers were suffering from were orchestrated by countries of Human Rights. All heads were for sale. But the wealthy asylum seekers who were under the protective umbrella of smugglers could cross the frontier of Spain-Morocco in all tranquility for four thousand Euros with falsified passports. They were crossing the border as if they were going to their bedrooms. They did not worry about anything that was happening to other travelers. They could melt themselves among those who were going to work behind the European fence. But the refugees who couldn't get this huge sum of four thousand Euros to cross the frontier by walking or in the dashboards and trunks of a car, and were considered as "economic migrants," who they stopped imperatively. And every halted head was subject for collective expulsion and the police was earning one hundred Euros by each head arrested. These captives, called "economic migrants," were fathers who the war had dispersed in the nature and nobody wanted to welcome them, because their physical quality and mental health were destroyed by the tons of bombs dropped on their countries. And some hundred thousand children dispatched throughout the world who only live by begging and become the princes in the kingdom of violence which the world does not want to talk about. Meanwhile, Samba Diallo, Little Boy, and many other kids were on Gurugu mountaintop, the forest. They were daily figuring how to brave the razor wire surrounding the Spanish enclave of Melilla in Morocco, probably the last step of their journey for safety. An average rock violently fell on Samba Diallo's right foot. His face contorted in pain as blood gushed up. Suddenly, he said, "I am freezing."

"You must be strong up here, the rocks hurt the feet and the cold can kill easily. Go under the shelter if you are freezing. This journey is not for kids like you guys," said the shelter mate.

"Has someone died up here before yesterday?" said Samba Diallo.

"Yes, and many people have died here, but you don't need to think about them. You should be focusing first on how to cross this border. Sorry for them. The dead are already dead, and they no longer care about what's happening behind them, likewise this perilous eternal journey. But from the temporary homes on Gurugu Mountain, the goal is so close; just below, you could see the lights of Melilla," said the shelter mate.

"When we will cross the border then?" said Samba Diallo.

"I have no idea. Someday, I hope so. Just wait patiently for the day of chance," said the shelter mate.

"How long have you been living up here?" said Samba Diallo.

"Almost two years and a half. I had boza (crossed the border) twice, climbing the razor wire but I have always been sent back here by Guardia Civils," said the shelter mate.

"Really! Why they sent you back here?" said Samba Diallo.

"I don't know. But this way in this journey to cross the border is a matter of chance and a matter of life and death," said the shelter mate.

However, the summertime was coming up slowly. And the spring was pushing winter out with its cocktail of cold. The winter supremacy used to collapse under the heat pressure that was coming up without ever giving any chance to the skiers to exercise their passion and make it pleasurable for the public. And people were weaving links with the beaches, swimmers were challenging themselves under the watchful eye of lifeguards. The sailboats were guided by the waves and the wind. But the drug barons were freely evacuating their cargoes in all safety to the same old Europe that was refusing to welcome the refugees. It was enough to pay the navy and the soldiers posted all along the shore to pass cannabis. On the other side of the strait on the literal shore, the houses of the drug leaders were at the beginning of the beaches in order to have easy access to the sea and strategize for the departure of the cannabis cargoes from Morocco to Europe. Everyone, from hashish traffickers to the coast soldiers, were usually corrupt. All the negotiations were done in the dark. There would be zodiacs filled with smuggled travelers and they would pass through the European channels unnoticed in the dark; the coast guards would show complete indifference to such illicit activities.

On the other hand, on the same Mediterranean Sea, the fishing boats and zodiacs overloaded with children used to multiply. Almost all these small boats used to get lost in the middle of the unlimited salty water of Mediterranean Sea. However, on the other side of the sea, the big strong boats with all the upper technology were coming from the powerful countries for the rescue of humans from the mouth of death. But the rescuers were oftentimes coming just after the shipwrecks. Most migrant boats used to capsize. Some humanitarian boats used to save a few people. Many nameless children were dying by asphyxiation in this salty water of the sea. And the entire world was surprisingly witnessing the strange silence of the world leaders in face of these multiple shipwrecks of over thirty thousand people at the bottom of the salty water of the sea between Italy and Libya. Despite the world financial crisis, the factories that used to make these floating coffins on the sea would never know poverty. And the radars and the thermal camera never detected the boats at the seaside. Furthermore, the little carpenters who were making these small fishing boats that were transporting refugees, without ever going through a port, would never know the economic crisis that was hitting the third world. From winter to spring, from spring to summer, and from summer to winter, some thousands of people would die under the eyes people who talked about Human Rights all day long. The poor refugees were being squeezed against each other and stowed like a needle pack in small boats mostly overloaded, all so the smugglers could gain as much monetary profit as they could yield through the strength; it did not matter as they would then starve the travelers in the forests or throw them into the water on the slightest misconduct. The water would carry them back to Algeria or another country; otherwise they would drown in the sea. They did not know they were paying the price of their shrouds, hoping to escape death while they were actually heading to their graves. They never reached their final destinations. And their journey turned into an eternal journey. Almost all these refugees ended up their journey in hell, hoping to get peace and security, in the deep misted and ebullient sea. And the Mediterranean Sea would turn into a cemetery for hopeless ones. And the disappearance of Little Boy became the cause of Samba Diallo's panic and sadness. Samba Diallo felt alone again in his journey. His journey turned into a fraternal mourning. Mourning over mourning. Samba Diallo blamed then the salty water of the sea for eating the dream of re-educating his friend and savior, Little Boy, in the desert. Sitting by the sea, the waves were coming up and were erasing on the fine sand the entire story of Samba Diallo's savior, in who was included the executioner and the victim, through manipulation. Samba Diallo wanted to sing his miserable life to forget his painful grieving in the silence, but the sea would never be able tell him where it had hidden the body of his friend, Little Boy. Just as Samba Diallo threw up the salty water of the sea from his lungs, his wrists were bound in handcuffs and he was subjected to collective deportation to the desert. Before leaving the forest, the Lieutenant had told him that he had been on duty in Congo and Rwanda as a Blue Helmet. The Lieutenant asked Samba Diallo first in Nigala, and then in Swahili. He wanted to know if Samba Diallo was from

Congo. Samba Diallo said that he could not speak either of these two languages. So, the Lieutenant added that "the Sub-Sahara is very vast, painted in green by its different types of forests, yellow by this immense ocean of sand we call Sahara, and blue by the sea that surrounds it on which we can see the different big fishing vessels and the gas plants that are constantly spitting fire. A land rich in the basement, but badly governed by its leaders who get the power by the way of guns, hurting their peoples under the influence of their former colonizers, who are in general the engines of the civil wars where millions of people get refuge in the horrible living conditions by escaping the different colors of massacres." In his speech, the Lieutenant seemed the only one of Maghreb who felt comfortable as an African in his Arab skin. But he knew more about the massacre of kids in north of Kivu, where kids worked under the menace of armed men. But he didn't dare say it. He just nodded his head before Samba Diallo got in a police car. But before getting deported, everyone had to taste the bitter taste of concentration camps. And these travelers were subsequently escorted under the police's surveillance. Only the military knew where they were going to throw away these travelers in their journey. The desert was the reliable place. None of these soldiers knew Samba Diallo's name. They gave him a nickname "bambino" because he was smaller and too young. Samba Diallo was one of the smallest travelers in this collective deportation group. All other travelers were looking at him wickedly because he was annoying them. He could not support the living conditions in which they were living. But, soldiers thought that Samba Diallo was a stubborn boy who was disobeying their instructions. They did not know yet his exile experience. When he would speak out on the mistreatment of his fellows along with his own, he would receive further punishment from the policemen. He did not know he was not allowed to rebel against the injustice and maltreatment being carried out. It seemed to him some other travelers arbitrarily detained knew that they don't make noises there. Then, they used to hate Samba Diallo for aggravating their sufferings. Some inmates used to draw the maps of their home countries to relive the great moments in their lives and getting bogged down in another mental depression by measuring the living conditions in which they used to live. It was during Ramadan, the fasting month, and according to the Islamic terminology everyone should abstain from eating and drinking during daylight hours. Samba Diallo picked up a piece of dry bread and ate it up to not die from hunger. A piece of bread could be found easily everywhere, in all corners of a street. The bread is the national and traditional food. But this dry bread was like adding fuel to the fire to his punishment. Samba Diallo had probably broken the law of traditional myth without knowing it.

On the collective expulsion day, one of the young auxiliary force member found Samba Diallo behind the van that was to serve as a vehicle to drive the detained ones to Nador's police office; these abuses, humiliations, and forced evictions of people against their wills, that the world leaders used to call "humanitarian return" while it was the deportation (they did not want to say the real name), said to Samba Diallo, "I had beaten a teenager the last time until he fainted. But I was under the influence of drugs when I was beating up this teenager. However, when I came back to myself, the scene of that crime remained engraved in my mind. And I became over and over addicted to the drugs to not see that scene again. Please don't judge me by my acts, I didn't want to lose my job, my only hope." The young auxiliary force seemed someone who was confessing his gestures. He wanted to add more things. But Samba Diallo did not want to listen to his detractor. Samba Diallo was painfully suffering from a back pain. And he was rather focused on this traumatic pain.

The iron curtain in front of which these travelers were getting beaten to death was the door of the Human Rights countries, and behind this scintillating barrier of barbed wire, there was a union of a powerful Club that had been there since decades. It seemed to be a united Club of twenty-eight inseparable members. The Club was composed of some kingdoms, a kingdom governed by a pretty queen with her beautiful crown, and some adventurers who used to plan all the time huge budgets to conquer the world, leaving some unforgettable souvenirs behind them—sometimes those that survived the horrifics of bombing and would never be able to forget the pain and mental and physical tortures they went through. The list of the Club was too long. Longer than a TGV to Madrid-Moscow.

However, the young girl, Nabila, was a descendant of a great labor father who had joined the nice and united Club during both world wars that destabilized the whole world. Some families came also from the four corners of the planet to join the same Club of twenty-eight members. Over the years, the Club grew. The Club, in its kindness, advocated freedom for all, no distinction, giving some wings to everybody to feel welcomed home. Then, Nabila decided to eil her face for her religion's sake. Her dress created a huge polemic discussion in the nice Club that was advocating freedom for all. Suddenly, the Club began to brutalize Nabila for wearing the burkini at the beach. On the other hand, Qataris rich oil tankers veiled from head to toes with their crowns on the heads were openly welcomed as heroes in the private residences, unrolling red carpet with a thunder of applause, kissing them on their feet. It was so hard to distinguish all these veiled people, whether a woman or a man. However, Nabila was married to Pascal since many years ago. She wasn't allowed in public places because of the veils she was wearing every day. She felt stigmatized in a society of "freedom for all." Her children did not eat that injustice. And they used to seek for every means to put carnages in public places forbidden to their mother for her justice. Notwithstanding that, everyone used to envy them, even all those who possessed all the riches at their reach, thanks to its power and its influence exercised around the world.

Meanwhile, in Southern Europe, an endless stream of hopeless refugees was fleeing the chemical attacks in the Syrian civil war and beginning their journey. The highways were blackened by helpless human nurseries with some souvenirs from their home country in their arms and on their heads. They used to debark every day by hundreds from different zodiacs on Greek Islands. Sometimes, accompanied by many children. The numbers were a lot but only those that were traveling could discern how many there actually were. They planned to be closer to the coasts and called this information "the doc." Some kids were dying by asphyxiation in the salty water of the sea as well. Many of the travelers preferred going to Libya despite the dangers of the civil war, in order to find a safe haven. News of the dead and the swirls and dangers of the sea could not deter this aim and they were unafraid of all kinds of threats. Likewise, refugees came from Sub-Saharan countries. And the world leaders used to call them "economic migrants." This earthquake of refugees has shaken the entire world, particularly Europe and its Union, from North to South and from East to West. This immigration issue was a spark that divided their Union. Some leaders wanted other European leaders to open up their borders for refugees but refused to welcome them themselves, leaving the homeless to suffer out on the streets as if they were not human. But that led to a reinforcement of frontiers. And the transit countries were putting their blackmails in execution. They too wanted to be respected honorably by the same European Union. The fate of the humans was no longer a priority. The solidarity term was just words written on a piece of paper; the reality showed people dying in pain instead of saving them. West of Europe, it seemed the refugee migration policy of Berlin was set up on a good foot. The refugees who were debarking on the Greek's peninsula would head to Germany. The people were witnessing then the journey of the human cattle. All trains were overloaded, heading to Germany. People were fleeing the Greek concentration camps for the open land of refugees in Berlin. Despite daily witnessing the nationalist uprisings to stop the crow invaders, "economic migrants," while they were being chased by the bombs dropped in Aleppo and other places, it seemed that Angela Merkel, the German conservative leader, had formally rejected these calls to questions about the nonreception of refugees in distress. She could not give up her humanitarian responsibility. She had opened her country gate to over a million refugees escaping the wars. But she was challenged by her own party and long-time opponents because of her policy to give a sharp turn to her immigration policy. At that time, the welcome of the refugees was becoming pretty much repugnant, like the anus of a civet. Nobody wanted to taste it. This call of humanitarian solidarity for refugees was a spark to the division of the world. The world was fissured forever in ten thousand pieces, and European Union was severely struck and divided by this immigration issue since the wind that had brought the sequels of the mistrust of the two world wars. And Europe completely forgot its Union façade and made do with meagre refugee camps rather than providing the refugees with better and equal opportunities. The world elite kicked Human Rights away and gave birth to a ruthless political machine that was crushing the life of millions. Almost all the powerful countries around the world started building walls at their borders. Nobody wanted to hear the salty shouts of kids in the salty water of the Mediterranean Sea.

After a deportation to the desert, Samba Diallo struggled again to join Rabat, the political capital of Morocco. He would wake up early morning and start his job of begging until evening, he and many other kids in their nightmare of his myth of European heaven in the storm and the cold fog under the pedestrian bridge that led to the faculty of medicine, crossing the railroad linking Rabat-Casablanca, second capital, just a few steps from the largest bus station. In the eyes of society, Samba Diallo and other kids were some beggar ants that could never stop begging. Samba Diallo was ashamed to beg at roundabouts with beggar mates looking for something to eat. He no longer wanted the society to call him "mesquin" (shabby). To the society, "to beg" is to be cursed by God, creator of universe. Samba Diallo had become one of the princes of violence. Endowed with his physical strength, he imposed the jungle law to the weak kids who could not defend themselves to face the urban violence. And these kids would respect him thanks to his physical strength. They considered him as a protector who was defending them from the machete wars, and the dark insecurity that reigned in the street.

During the city cleaning operation, the ghetto was broken. And Samba Diallo was welcomed by a charitable organization and conducted to a refugee office. He left the bus station to Takaddoum, crumbling buildings, behind a long car ride north of the center of Morocco's capital, Rabat, and its *souk* (market) through a maze of narrow alleys in a densely populated northern suburb, where illegal sub-Saharan migrants shared tea, swapping stories of assault, rape, and daily encounters with hostility. Where respect was almost non-existent. An unemployed young one under the influence of drugs, most of these adult illiterates, and the presence of what seemed to be a large influx of people from elsewhere was causing real tensions in a neighborhood gilded already with violence. A hopeless youthfulness of a country in the process of loss, ravaged by the epidemic large-scale traffic of hashish, where all confusions were revolving at the ringtones of machetes. However, Samba Diallo was already a veteran of violence and the reprisals of police. So, he did not care about the

:hreats made by these young people. Even when they used :o brandish machete under his eyes. He was greatly welcomed in this block of "Who can live." Samba Diallo was housed with many other illegal migrants in a rootless, windlowless building. An insalubrity building, no electricity nor potable water, but rented to them by smugglers. Some used water bottles were used for the daily shower, and for any kind of restroom, they only had a bucket of water to wipe themselves and no means to flush the dirty water, which gave off an unbearable odor. These travelers used to call themselves "squatters." A community living. As soon as Samba Diallo arrived at Takaddoum, he was attacked with a machete one night.

"Give me your whole lot *flouze* now (money in Arabic), *mon ami*, otherwise you'd get a stab in belly," said the aggressor.

"You can own my whole body, otherwise I don't have a penny for you, *khoya*. If I could sell you right now to buy a piece of bread, I would do it," replied Samba Diallo.

"I would slice your head up if you dare say that again, *mesquin*," said aggressor.

"Do not call me, *mesquin*, otherwise you'd see my punch up," said Samba Diallo.

"*Hein!* Little asshole, if you dare challenge me on my territory, you would pay for the consequences," said the aggressor, brandishing a machete.

"*Handek khoya* (be careful man), I am not strong enough to challenge but if you touch one of my hair, you'd know who I am," said Samba Diallo, always ready to fight back.

Then, a fierce fight got triggered in this chock-a-block crumbling buildings. Samba Diallo got a stab on his left vertebral column and the aggressor got a bleeding nose. "I'd let you go today because I'm suffering from this fatal stab I got on my vertebral column, but you better keep me in mind because I'll never ever forget you," Samba Diallo said furiously, leaving the curious spectators.

The next day, the aggressor ran towards Samba Diallo and said, "You were aggressed yesterday, correct?"

"Yes, I was violently aggressed yesterday evening. So?" said Samba Diallo.

"It was me. You know why?" said the aggressor.

"No, I don't," said Samba Diallo.

"Welcome to my sector. You're my friend from today until death. Look over there, it is my older brother, Mehdi, who's selling ingredients for sauce. In case you need some, please come over and get some," said the aggressor, going to his brother's place.

Pending the processing of his asylum application, Samba Diallo stressed out the charitable organization that welcomed him to find a public school for him. Because many sheets that were provided to him by these different international organizations sometimes crumpled when folded, and could not allow him to go back to any public school. This time, Samba Diallo's long-awaited wishes to maintain his studies on a solid wheel were heard by Mustafa who had grown up in Europe. Mustafa decided then to sign Samba Diallo up in his culinary school among a hundred children left behind by the society. Mustafa did not want to know him nor see him before. He rather wanted to help Samba Diallo and participate actively in the education of this teen. But the culinary school was in another city, Salé, near Rabat. About 20 minutes away by a taxi. More than an hour of walk. And Samba Diallo used to cross Rabat to join Salé (city) on other side of river Bou Regreg every day. But, Samba Diallo's first time at this culinary school was a seismic atmosphere. Ebola epidemic virus was dramatically ravaging in West Africa. And when other teens were looking at him, they thought automatically about the Ebola virus. Samba Diallo was clothed and swollen by the coat of a veteran that a bodyguard had given to him for cold. Everyone used to look at him as if he was a big doll fallen from the sky sitting upstairs. Matter of fact, Samba Diallo was a partridge with hard legs in a family farm of yellow ducklings. All these teens thought they were superior to Samba Diallo. And Samba Diallo did not care about that matter.

Culinary School was the only chance for Samba Diallo to leave the street because there was less opportunity such as Takaddoum El Youssoufia, J5 etc. in many cities. And it was easy to see women in needs in these crowded neighborhoods knocking on the broken doors and asking, "*Toi, veut travail?*" using the broken French. (Do you want work?) Which meant, do you want to have sex with me? If anyone answered back with a question, "What does *toi, yeut travail* mean?" it was a sign that meant the person was new in the ghetto.

Prostitution is illegal; one cannot see these women in the streets as in other countries, but it took to live in the ghetto to know that this evil was legal the whole night. And when one heard "*c'est tombé*" or "*c'est* free" while it was not dinner time yet, meant someone's mother had come to sell herself to feed her kids. It was heart-wrenching for Samba Diallo when a woman who was older than his genetic umbrella hopelessly told him that she was doing it to feed her kids, while he was another mother's son who was figuring out how to feed himself. Every morning, Samba Diallo was waking up with empty stomach to go to class, knowing that he did not want to be a blue cordon. Cuisine was not his big passion, likewise pastry. There were only these two choices. So, Samba Diallo decided then to take the pastry class not to feel alone in the violence.

Meanwhile, Eid-al-Adha, also called the "Festival of Sacrifice," the second of two Islamic holidays celebrated worldwide each year, and considered the holier of the two, honoring the willingness of Ibrahim to sacrifice his son as an act of obedience to God's command, was coming up slowly. And the cattle markets were filled with sheep and were also bleating almost in all the yard. However, the culinary school's principal had given some gifts for holiday to all his students. But Fatima wanted more than what she got and wondered if Samba Diallo would give his to her. Samba Diallo flatly refused to give her his gift. Fatima was furious. She became redder than before. Her slave had just disobeyed her. She felt reduced at zero degree. In her eyes, Samba Diallo was incarnating the old century pictures of Bilal, the first Muezzin and slave. And she said something that hurt Samba Diallo deeply. She said, "Dirty son of negro, ancestors cursed by the sun gods. That's the reason why you are also burned such as you are." She said that with satisfaction.

A few youths were shocked and encouraged Samba Diallo to react. "Come on, react fat shit, have a heart in your chest instead of an anus," said a crowd of teens and another wave of mockeries followed.

Another response came up from the crowd. "Go away, band of tramps, I won't react badly under your influences. My genetic umbrella told me I should respect any feminine gender. So, I don't want to use my strength of predator to break this girl's jaw, who has just disrespected me, only to delight you, band of tramps because you are so happy when you do call me '*mon ami*' also, and you do get angry when I do call you '*mon ami*.' I can't disrespect any words from my genetic umbrella. Make me a way, I have to go," said Samba Diallo, leaving the crowd.

"You better go, it would be good for you," said a voice in the crowd.

"Hey, Fatima, don't talk to Samba Diallo like that, he is one of us," said another voice in the crowd.

"I don't care if he is your half," said Fatima.

"Leave her alone, man, she can do whatever she wants, I don't care. I merely wish her all happiness and see her succeeding, and out from her daily misery," said Samba Diallo.

"I have to go, I don't want to waste my time dealing with you guys. I am under another arrest warrant for having robbed your religion. People usually shoot me down with my own belief. They do consider me as a *Houdhy*, 'non-Muslim.' They think that they are more Muslim than me. The same question used to come back to me every time. Are you Muslim? I was born in a Muslim family and raised in a Muslim tradition," said Samba Diallo once again while going home.

Samba Diallo was hurt by her words but he controlled himself in order to protect Fatima. He knew that the culinary school may have been Fatima's only hope, as it was for other children, for if he were to tell on her, she may be kicked out of school. He realized that after this, Fatima would be left with no choice but to sell herself in order to survive out in the world. Sometimes, despair pushes people to become weak when they don't know how to protect themselves.

After a few months of waiting with the ideas of frequent suicide attempts in his head, Samba Diallo was recognized as a refugee by the refugee office on January 30, 2015. In the refugee office, Samba Diallo could hear from the interlocutor telling that he had a duty to go back to school, the right not to be abused in different construction sites by doing the hard works that could bend his back. And the interlocutor added that children had a particular protection, citing the Geneva Convention as illustration. The interlocutor had also told Samba Diallo about a long line of children's rights, but Samba Diallo could only remind back that he would be back on the school benches. With this good news in Samba Diallo's head, he left refugee Office, going back to Takaddoum between the sky and the Earth, making some rotations on the grass under the rain, with the document "To whom it may concern." That day was shortest throughout Samba Diallo's journey. He could not catch up all thousands of insomnia days in their roofless building, but he thought that it would have little change in his living condition. However, the days were rapidly flying one after another. And the charity organization that had put Samba Diallo on his feet, giving him a human face, a dignity. Specially, this lady who was so nice, Ms. Aminah, who had allowed him to throw out all thoughts, relieving his heart from all the pains housed in it. Her sweet words like ice on the heart of Samba Diallo, who could make him dream during the one-on-ones of psychological session. Ms. Aminah had a simplicity to describe the life by making Samba Diallo believe that everything could go well. She used to make Samba Diallo want to live again every time she planned on an appointment with him. And Samba Diallo wanted to keep on hearing the sweet words from Ms. Aminah to forget his pains. But the charity organization sadly told Samba Diallo that it could not take care of him anymore because he was already a refugee, saying, "You are already under the international protection, we must take care of someone else." Samba Diallo seemed visibly paralyzed by that news. But he had to accept it against his will because the decision had already been taken. Samba Diallo was so sad when he was leaving the charity organization office with his sheet on which all children's rights was written down and underlined. Samba Diallo wanted to burn this sheet of his life. He felt he was under the international protection of UNHCR but that little piece of paper was not enough and it held other issues. He thought he was under international umbrella, protected by an international organization, but his dream to go back to school didn't come true and UNHCR didn't go anything. He returned to Takaddoum, where violence was a volcano in boiling that fed itself on abandonment. Where one could read despair on all the faces, pain lines, and scars hidden behind some tattoos. Symbols of a lifetime on bodies that were the real works of art, not to forget the daily pains.

Every tattoo was heavy with meaning, an eternal memory of a long journey of life. But Samba Diallo still believed in his pen. That could get him out of the darksome nights of his journey. With his backpack on his back, he used to breathe the smell of chalk through the door when passing in front of the schoolyards. He would use any papers he would find in the streets to write down on. Some people thought that he was going to school somewhere. Yet, the violence was his daily routine and when he would tell people he wanted to be a writer, they would laugh at him because of his appearance and living conditions.

In the quest of returning to school, Samba Diallo fell into the ambush of the drug dealers. An embarrassing situation in which it was impossible to refuse their proposals. Refusing their proposals meant digging one's own grave on a mountaintop. Samba Diallo could not hesitate to accept such proposals. It was also useless to resist them. He complied with the jungle law to avoid the menaces and moral reprisals. He got enlisted in drug trafficking, a rentable and well-organized business. An environment where money and good conscience could not be cooked very well together. The misery, many roll of bills, and famished unconsciousness mixed together in the same sack and showed to an unemployed young in a crumbling building and poorest neighborhood, always led to an excessive violence against neighbors. Samba Diallo made himself a place and was going to be the child prodigy for the dealers. Under his hood of little dealer, he used to shake hands with his former tormentors, police, and eat around a same table. Interest was tying them together, and they used to meet each other. Endowed with his enormous talent of dealing, Samba Diallo was solicited. It was necessary to note all entries and exits of the drug to a corporate accountant. Good accounts made good friends. Samba Diallo was going to be a real penny machine that could put all the banknotes in the pockets of his hawks. His daily salary was depended on his daily sale. He used to risk ending up with a bullet in his head forever. Samba Diallo preponderance used to put many banana skins on his way (a lot of enemies). He was in a hole where nobody could hear him. The duration of his shabby life was only counting on the tip of a simple pistol. It could be abbreviated before he was eighteen years old in a banal discussion. The sacred law of silence was a code that could not be broken. One had to respect the rules despite the fact that death was omnipresent. It was really a miracle when a chick survived between the claws of a hawk. It was useless to talk about justice to someone who applied the code of justice. Money was heavier in the balance between justice and truth. It was useful to sue someone when one knew that the complaint could be a poison against ourselves. But Samba Diallo just wanted to leave this violent and bloodthirsty place where the prostitution of minors was a big flourishing business, thanks to the complicity established by those who were making the orders to round off their end of the month. These prostitutes and victims of human traffickers could do their jobs thanks to the provisions set up. However, Samba Diallo did not want someone else to read him a court order in a prison as his birthday gift. He decided then to send a letter to the refugee officer to know if someone could remember him still.

Dear Protective Umbrella

"The violence made me flee my birth home, but the violence has not forgotten me yet. The environment in which I do live rhymes with violence, many aggressions, the blooming is conditionally restrained, and liberty is confiscated. Delivered to myself, I'm daily fighting against all problems of the streets. I am exposcd to this huge cold from the distant blue sea. Those with whom I share the same painful suffering let me know through words that I am not one of them. They throw cruel words at my face all day long. Only a few words from the novels that I borrow often leave on my lips a few bursts of smiles. Viewing all these obstacles that I endured throughout my perilous long journey, if my protective umbrella does not protect me, I risk losing my life someday from all these obstacles."

Thank you for taking your time to read my letter carefully, or sincerely.

Samba Diallo

Towards the end of fourth hour of the afternoon, Samba Diallo got a call from the refugee office. On the line, a feminine voice said, "We please you to go to the Center for refugees." And the next morning, Samba Diallo started walking to find this center for refugees, asking unknowns on the street, between the influx of vehicles and these drivers who would stop in middle of two-ways and begin long greetings with pedestrians without caring for those behind them, and when asked to move along, they would acknowledge their requests with insults in return.

"*Salam, khoya!* (Hi, man). Do you know where the Center for refugees is located?" asked Samba Diallo.

"*Mon ami*, go straight, at a half mile, turn left at the first traffic light, the Center for refugees is on your right," said the unknown interlocutor.

"*Chokran, khoya* (thank you, man), for your help," said Samba Diallo.

Samba Diallo got this destination but the Center for refugees wasn't there. He headed forward to someone else.

"*Salam, khoya!* Do you know where the Center for refugees is?"

"Center for refugees, Center for refugees, go a little bit straight. Then, left turn at roundabout and you'll see your destination," said the unknown interlocutor.

After a day of questioning, Samba Diallo finally found the Center for refugees after some long hours of walking. The days were following one after the other and Samba Diallo started another process with Refugee and Stateless Office to re-analyze his documents for getting a residence card, the visa for a new normal life. The residence card that was considered as the passport of a refugee's life did not allow him to access public schools. The problems of administrative documents followed him everywhere. The tourists who were going on vacation taught the refugees some English, Spanish, and German words and were also profiting from refugees' kindness and good moods by stealing pictures and interviews to make documentaries. But they forgot about the anonymity instructions. To fight against the language barrier of his new life of refugee, they taught Samba Diallo and many refugee teens the host country language one hour a week, four hours a month. The repetition could be pedagogical, but it became frustrating they wanted to learn a lot of things about the world but they made them repeat over and over the same lesson for years. In addition, it seemed that the inter-culturality was one of the mottos and a battle weapon for the heads of reception at the refugees' Center, but Samba Diallo hated the Center for refugees because of the painting exhibitions of the sufferings of their border crossing. Especially, Ms. Nickname, when she'd send him into hell, turning on a video of more than an hour. A video in which boats filled with children in distress were capsizing on the Mediterranean Sea. And with her timer, she would come back in her office when the video would just be ending up and asking, "Kids, who can conclude what he learned from the films?"

A hand rose up.

"Yes, you," said Ms. Nickname.

"I could tell you that I saw actually how my friend, Little Boy, died from asphyxiation in middle of the salty water of Mediterranean Sea," said Samba Diallo and stayed quiet.

Ms. Nickname did not know she was lighting an unsupportable pain in Samba Diallo. She compelled him to tell more about his friend, Little Boy. Samba Diallo stayed silent. He did not like being pressurized into telling something that he did not want to tell.

"What do you need from me?" asked Ms. Nickname.

"Nothing, I just need a forever mother who can be a shoulder on which I can cry," said Samba Diallo.

"Alright, do you have a dream?" said Ms. Nickname.

"Yes, like everyone has," said Samba Diallo.

"What are you going to do in the future?" said Ms. Nickname.

"Well, I'm going to write about my miserable days someday," said Samba Diallo happily.

"Writing?" said Ms. Nickname, laughing.

"Yes, writing. I want to transform my negative thoughts into positive thoughts through lines by honoring all sacrifices done by my genetic umbrella for giving to me all opportunities to learn and defend myself someday," said Samba Diallo.

"Writing is for smart and genius people. You better choose another job than staying always in your tears. Writing is not a job," said Ms. Nickname.

"Yes, I know, but, in my culture, one of the legends says that if we dream someday to scintillate like a star in a society of our siblings or others, we must take our chances and shoot awkwardly into the moonlight, in hopes that we may achieve what we dream of. In case we unluckily miss the moonlight, we could stay glued on the sky and scintillate sooner or later as a star because nothing ventured nothing gained. And if we had already chosen to dream about a lot bigger than a simple dream, then it is necessary to stay focused on this dream line hung in a void," said Samba Diallo.

"Courage! When we don't quit, we win," said Ms. Nickname.

"Thank you, I'm going to put my mind to it even if I am weakened now but it is not my fear. My fear is my world that's melting around me. I am alive but deeply hurting and my passion for writing is the only way I can heal this pain housed on my broken heart. But I don't know how to begin for the lack of writing skills. I have some ideas but I am afraid of being rejected by the publishers. And if there is no one to encourage me and I do not take the first step, my dream would never come true; like a shy girl who secretly loves someone but does not dare tell him, afraid of how the society would react," said Samba Diallo.

However, the little secret that Ms. Nickname didn't know, writing for Samba Diallo was to run away from the demons that were gnawing him inside. Writing was to flee away from the real world and live in an inventive world where nobody could see him fighting against his mental depression. Writing was to flee his mental disaster by avoiding suicide. Writing was to shout in a desert where nobody could hear him and forget his self-fulfillment in order to hear the voices of others and unearth these voices buried in the silence that were left behind. It also was a great remedy to his immense loneliness, stress, and sadness, and that also kept the nightmares at bay. And to sleep with eyes open without seeing tomorrow. Samba Diallo had fallen in love with literature. Even if everything was to melt around him, he felt like living in this inexistent landscape believing that the literary wing could blow him away from the real world and his deepest pain.

At the same time, Samba Diallo was getting some messages from the drug dealers. They needed him still. He had the art to persuade customers. The circle of gays used to compliment him also all day long that he was handsome. They wanted just what interested them. They didn't care about his miserable life. They used to flatter him with some big blue bill of Dirham, Moroccan money. Some renamed cougars would propose him some money to taste the honey of their old age. And some religious dignitaries wanted to see him taking a greyhound class with them for a short privacy moment against a ransom. The Hashish resin smell used to pollute the air. But Samba Diallo believed in himself and his pen. He used to prefer to be a slave to his literary thoughts than to be under any domination for a single day's happiness of all these human sharks who were taking part in his destruction. Any experimented lifeguard couldn't prevent him from drowning in his literary alcoholism. For his safety, Samba Diallo wondered to his international umbrella to take him away from the mouth of these inhuman predators. He wanted to break this deadly silence that was traumatizing him mentally. The answer to his request was an embellished phrase when he heard "We don't have the national police at our disposal to ensure the safety of everyone" from his international umbrella. Yet, everyone makes a little error in his life. But Samba Diallo's error was in telling the truth about the people who were using him to distribute drugs. Every time, his international umbrella used to question him about drug legislation. While the question was easier to respond, Samba Diallo was confused between legal and illegal. Both words were finished by "al." He could not choose one. After the partial analysis of his controversial past, his international umbrella decided to confine him in one of the housing of protection for minor's safety. But that safe house was a hell for Samba Diallo when he was starved under that safe roof of his international umbrella. Moreover, all his steps were in Farad's hands, a drunkard neighbor who had phobia of a "*mon ami*" and he was an iconic figure who used to hate Azi (negro). When this drunkard was intoxicated, he allowed himself to insult all neighbors and attacked all passersby before he felt comfortable in his flesh. And he would use Samba Diallo's door as a xylophone with the alcohol bottle and the window was breaking by bottle pressures. To hang out, Samba Diallo would oftentimes bribe Farad and would finally have some freedom.

Cut off from the outside world, and sitting in that housing, Samba Diallo would keep going in triangles, from his bedroom to the kitchen to the toilet; being confined in the house, it was his only routine. Covered by his pain, he felt frustrated from being held captive under a roof. However, the date of the New Year meeting was coming up. All teens were hoping to go back again to school. Mido used to tell him everything that was happening outside. She had fled the violence in Goma, capital city of the North Kivu province in the Eastern Democratic Republic of the Congo. She also wanted to go back to school like billions of children across the world. But the residence cards and tons of documents of the international rights that had been distributed to these teens were just decoration to embellish them. The last meeting was a big hope for them. But it was not enough to merely exploit their weaknesses, they went ahead and coaxed them to come to the meetings by offering them a meal at the end of the day; this the children readily accepted as they were always hungry. All of them would respond to the message in a second for the meeting. In the meeting, almost the whole world was present—the representative of the Swiss ambassador and his daughter, the minister of the foreign affairs, some local authorities, the different non-governmental organizations, and the children's rights defenders. It was a golden opportunity for

Samba Diallo to explain the large-scale illiteracy rate of the children that he had seen during his long journey. Furthermore, the meeting was based on the future of the refugee children on the soil of their host countries. Samba Diallo, considered as the rude child, wanted to talk about what he had lived through and saw, the scourge of illiteracy which too many children were suffering from. But men in suits did not want to listen to his crazy thoughts, to what they did not see sitting in their air-conditioned offices. They wanted Samba Diallo to praise them, like a griot does. Teens were suffering and continuing to suffer in the silence from physical and mental violence, girls were suffering from sexual harassment on the street. But, when Samba Diallo asked a question about the young refugees' education, the question could not wait a second to get its answer. There was no good sense of humor about "equality" that His Majesty the King Mohamed VI was advocating in the voice of spokesman of the authorities of integration and education. He said, "When Moroccan workers went to Europe, they started working on the construction sites." He did not know yet that Samba Diallo was one of the potential teen laborers, the cheaper demolishers who were sleeping on construction sites in the cold. In addition, he added, "You should now start working like Moroccans who worked in the 20th century, to be integrated into the European society." It was a big cold shower for these teens who were waiting to find a solution to their illiteracy problems. Also, Luna, the representative for children's rights was upset by the long series of ambiguous comparison from the spokesman but she had to respect his point of view because freedom of speech was allowed for all. Even Samba Diallo could have liked to work at a less cost in the construction sites like Moroccan workers in Europe to repay that debt of inhuman forced laborers inflicted on thousands of Moroccan workers. That would not stop any of these teens to think about their futures. The only thing burning their hearts was this national education policy that was slowing down his dream to go back to a public school because of a piece of paper. Well, as in Samba Diallo's culture, a kid could not retort to his elder. But Samba Diallo broke this myth of his tradition because it was about his future, the future of all these kids who were facing many obstacles to eventually go die on the sea. Then, he held his speech with incorrect spellings in his right hand, a crumpled paper between his fingers. At the beginning, he was a little bit scared. All eyes were on the little *Azi* that he was. Men in suits, ties, and black shiny shoes. Some women were dressed in long dresses that covered their whole bodies and the sails that were covering their long black hair. Samba Diallo could see their eyes, noses, and their mouths that were occasionally visible through the fabric. On the other hand, women coming from the other side of Mediterranean Sea were dressed in pants like men. They talked about school for "all children" and children's rights. Samba Diallo braved his fear of authorities and his shyness, and let them know all children did not have the same rights. But he forgot to mention that all children left behind by the society had just needed a smile, a look, a gesture before seeing this peace hidden behind their sad faces.

"We are the damned ones of this society the poor fruits of the beginning of the drought of our time that did not have the time to ripen well in this end of the world. We are hildren condemned of this century, those that the world doesn't want to see. A lost generation, for whom death doesn't matter in the quest of liberty. Any life has a price, the price of endless journeys, of forgetfulness, and of massive eradications at the mercy for those sexually obsessed. We are muffled shouts in the sea, yet the strongest teens for facing the claws of the night; we are the human sacrifices in the history of humanity offered to the sharks of the Mediterranean Sea. We are the brave ones confronting the razor wires, running away from the daily violence. We are millions of kids left behind by this ill society, heirs of the mental traumas which we are not the genitors of. In the history of antiquity, there are some laws that protect people. But we are the ones who do not matter in these laws. While there are several possibilities to welcome us, to act, and to open hands to us instead of cutting off our hands and twisting them in the salty water of the Mediterranean Sea. Some closed hearts that kill us silently. These hearts that preferred to let us die by drowning in the sea, forgetting that there were many kids of all ages, as theirs, among us. We are thousands of armed bodies of courage, a thousand kids with broken hearts who need forever mothers who can protect us, and live our childhood lives like all children of this world. Waiting for the whole world to listen to our stressed voices, we would be those who would daily be struggling for better tomorrow between the claws of the smugglers who abuse us physically and mentally by prostituting us.

"On my TV screen, I heard about the Child Rights. I wanted to meet them, but the opportunity to meet them was never granted to me. I would like to beg them to revise the

Geneva Convention about children's rights adopted by United Nations, November 20th, 1989. The protection of the children against harm is only a well-developed thesis with beautiful rhythms included in the wonderful paragraphs, covered with beautiful folders. But, the reality is dissimulated behind the guns. Long before, I joined my voices to the voices of the children of the whole world, a voice which everyone was only pretending to listen to behind their façade of humanitarian help, and inclining before the memories of all those unfortunate thousands of dead children drowned in the sea. I will go see the Supreme Pontiff and beg him to pray to the Almighty when he'd have free time for thousands of kids, for the genocide on the Mediterranean Sea in front of the door of the Chapel of Rome. We will never finish counting the numbers of nameless faces extinguished in this Mediterranean salt water," said Samba Diallo.

"How many kids are dying from hunger and thirst in anonymity? How many children still live in despair? How many are still under the influence of these fearsome assassins? How many children are begging on the crossroads to survive? How many hearts are broken by the claws of these smugglers? How many traumatized children are getting lost in nothingness? How many are afraid of retaliation and say nothing? How many are holding the weapons on their shoulders? How many will carry a gun?

"To sum up, when forests burn and animals line up and come to us for help, there would always be volunteers and vets to treat them with tolerance, civility, acceptance, dignity, and all needs, but when houses are burning and people in need are coming to us for help, the great defenders

104

Human Rights dehumanize their fellow men with all ean words, as if they are not humans like them.

"When will the international justice talk about these rned children, mothers, and fathers in battlefields and otect victims who flee violence?"

CPSIA information can be obtained
at www.ICGtesting.com
Printed in the USA
FSHW022130121219
64728FS